MEN
MAGNIFYING
MANHOOD

STORIES THAT GIVE HOPE
AND
EMPOWERMENT

MEN
MAGNIFYING
MANHOOD

STORIES THAT GIVE HOPE AND
EMPOWERMENT

CALVIN ELLISON, PHD

Ordering Information

Quantity sales. Special discounts are available on quantity purchases by corporations, associations, and others. Orders by trade bookstores and wholesalers. Please contact Dr. Ellison at dr.calellison@gmail.com

Editor
Lita P. Ward, The Editorial Midwife
LPW Editing & Consulting Services, LLC
www.litapward.com

Publisher
Published in the United States of America by
Ellisons Consulting Services LLC

ISBN: 978-0-578-51542-7

ENDORSEMENTS

"I am so glad Dr. Ellison decided to collaborate with other men and put together a book like this. The topic is very relevant and will help so many men on their journey to live out their purpose. This book is a game changer for men around the world!"

Sheena
Financial Parent Consultant
Financial Parent Academy

"Dr. Calvin Ellison is such a resource to the community. He provides knowledge and wisdom in the most critical areas of a man's life. I'm very happy to work closely with him as we both serve in the leadership of the Atlanta Black Chambers. He is definitely one of the foremost thought leaders in the realm of physical, mental, and spiritual health. This book is a gift to all of us. We've been so challenged in this process as males who need to realize our full potential.

It's time to magnify manhood!"

Melvin M. Coleman, MBA
Executive Director, Atlanta Black Chambers
384 Northyards Blvd N.W.
Bldg. 100
Atlanta, Ga. 30313
Office 877-964-6222 ext. 101
Cell 678-548-5242
www.atlantablackchambers.org

"Men Magnifying Manhood should be a part of anyone's library. When GOD said let us make man, Dr. Calvin Ellison heeded the call. Man is more than just flesh and blood; the complete man is mind body and spirit. Dr. Ellison, an anointed man of GOD, and his contributing writers have contributed spiritual insight in the areas of what it takes to magnify the manhood of men. Attributes such as maturity, responsibility, discipline, and commitment are just a few of the areas which he shares insight. This read should inspire the prodigal sons in the community to return home and assume their rightful place as leaders in the home and the community. Remember knowledge is the new currency. A must read!"

Calvin Maddox
Vice-President, Business Development
Atlanta Black Chambers

***

"Dr. Calvin Ellison has envisioned a masterpiece to empower men from all walks of life! This is a MUST read for any man who needs insight and encouragement. The powerful testimonials in this book will allow you to see how each man deals with life from a different perspective, build your faith, and assist one's journey on his path to manhood."

Walt Harris
NFL Player/Philanthropist/Motivational Speaker
Founder of Official Pro Players, Inc.

"To take on the responsibility of addressing men's issues is a big thing. I appreciate Dr. Ellison and the men who have joined him for seeing the need to empower males. I believe this book is the foundation for others that will help men be all they can be."

Henrietta Turnquest
Lawyer, Former GA Representative

"A delightful guide full of important healthy choices for those of us who want to enjoy the blessings of life. Dr. Calvin Ellison, has highlighted eloquently the significance of health by providing simple solutions to good eating and creating a balance with daily exercise."

Uzma A. Khan
Owner of Symponia Hospice
Executive Director, Official Pro Players

"Dr. Calvin Ellison now gives an inspirational look at the philosophy of "Men Magnifying Men." Man is both material and spiritual and this book is a marvelous combination of the two. This book will lead men to self-respect while helping one to distinguish between self-respect and self-conceit."

George G. Hill
Centers for Disease Control and Prevention (CDC)

"I can truly say that my husband is a "man for men." He has implemented what manhood is in our marriage and family for over 36 years. I am so proud that he has brought together a coalition of great men to address the important issue of manhood."

Dr. Judy Ellison
Author, Women's Coach

CONTENTS

FOREWORD

There are many books written that give insight into manhood from an individual perspective. Dr. Calvin Ellison has provided the reader with a different viewpoint from a multitude of men. Society has magnified many ideologies of masculinity. As boys take their journey into manhood, it is essential they receive the truth about what masculinity is, and the tools needed to equip one on their journey. The various perspective that highlight men in this book will minimize the stereotypes of what it takes to be a man. Each story magnifies each individual's journey to manhood and will challenge, direct, and empower readers to develop balanced perspectives of what it takes to be a man. *Men Magnifying Manhood* is a great mentoring tool that boys and men will benefit from in their day to day lives. Every age is a transitional phase that requires direction, knowledge, and most of the all the truth. Many men settle with the status quo of being a male. This read will raise the bar by inspiring young men to raise higher standards of living and thinking as mighty men applying Godly principles. Although this read aims its focus on young boys and men, women can also gain insight and understanding as wives and mothers to better support and build productive relationships with the men in their lives.

Walt Harris

NFL Player/Philanthropist/Motivational Speaker Founder of Official Pro Players, Inc.

INTRODUCTION

Everything was designed to have a conception, evolutionary process and maturation. As humans God created us to be His representatives, for the purpose of His pleasure and have stewardship over what is visibly seen (Psalms 8:6). As males, God's intention for us is to emerge from the womb, be nurtured, molded and led into manhood; with all its roles and responsibilities for the maturation for males.

But wait a minute; there is a problem! Many homes have no father in them. Countless males have no men to mentor them. Hurting, uncared for and confused boys roam our streets and fill our jails, longing to be guided in to true manhood. The desire is in them to be real men because God put it there. A male's greatest fulfillment comes from being the man God created him to be.

This book is the result of a group of men who said, "Enough is enough!" We will come together. We will work together. We will deal with why many males never experience the Promised Land of Meaningfulness, Maturation and Manhood. We will shine the light of our collective experiences, education and evolutions to make the journey of life brighter for every male we possibly can. Hence, you have in your hands: "Men Magnifying Manhood."

~ Calvin Ellison, PhD

GOD MAGNIFYING MANHOOD

Genesis 1:26

Job 7:17

Psalm 8:4-6

Biography of Calvin Ellison, PhD

Calvin Ellison, PhD is an Apostle, Author, Naturopathic Doctor, Certified Nutritional Consultant, Radio Host, Global Wellness Trailblazer and Marriage and Men's Advisor. He is the Founder of several Networks: the Kingdom Advancers Network of Churches and Businesses, Heirs Together Marriage Enrichment Network, the Vibrant Living Group, and the Men's Empowerment Network. He has also served on the Farmville, NC Economic Development Council, the North Carolina Institute of Medicine Committees, the North Carolina Mental Health Task Force and the Community Outreach Network Board of Eastern North Carolina.

While pastoring for 20 years, he is a constant presenter at Community Colleges, Universities and Businesses on various topics from Health and Wellness, Community Engagement, and Personal and Professional Growth. He has worked with such groups as the NC Office of Minority Health and Health Disparities (as its State-Wide Coordinator of two Health Programs), the Town of Farmville, NC as a Health Consultant, the National Kidney Foundation, the Health Start Foundation, North Carolina Department of Health and Human Services Women's Health Branch, Health Departments, Community-Based Organizations and Local Churches.

Dr. Calvin Ellison is the author of five books and co-author of five national publications. Together he and his wife have ministered in ten different countries. They have been married for 36 years and have three children and seven grandchildren.

Personal Profile

Key Words

Beyond, Create, Innovative, Wow, Imagine

Favorite Quote

"Making things happen to create new realities."

Values

Equitable Relationships, Networking, Empowering Others, Changing the Status Quo, Visionary Thinking

Marketable Skills

Public Speaking, Organizing, Leading, Networking, Continued Learning

Contact Information

Email: dr.calvinellison@gmail.com

Website: www.doctorcalvinellison.com

LinkedIn.com: Dr. Calvin Ellison

Facebook: Facebook.com/calvin.ellison.39

ROOT CAUSES OF THE MALE CRISIS

Calvin Ellison, PhD

It is an understatement to say there is a crisis among males. Boys are in crisis everywhere. Many live fatherless lives. Academically, in many developed nations they are falling behind. Scores of teenage males are focusing on gangs versus finishing school and going to college. In city after city, homes are abandoned by men who told their wife he loved her, helped raise the children but seemed to run out of the will power to keep leading.

According to Webster's dictionary, a "crisis" is a situation that has reached a critical phase. Looking at the state of males and men in today's society, we are in a crisis. We have moved from being confident about our identity to confusion about who we are and our purpose. Males have shifted from being respectful to the older men to treating many less than their age. Our prisons are full of fathers, uncles, nephews and sons.

In order to change "what is," we must look at "what is" for what it is. Is "what is" what you are willing to accept and tolerate?

3

Is "what is" what you want to live with and pass on to others? If not, then it is time we, in the words of Michael Jackson, "Look at the man in the mirror" and decide that change begins today; starting with you. Yes, you! You can be better. You can make a difference. You can motivate a teenager to stay in school, encourage a husband to be a better lover to his wife or a father, to be a true nurturer, model and guide to his children.

Let your life be a story that gives hope and empowerment to a brother looking for help and a man determined to be better. I want you to look with me at what I consider to be three of the major root causes of the male crisis. Just three. I am aware that there are others, but let's talk about the three I personally am passionate about dealing with.

CRISIS #1 – IDENTITY

Who are you? Where and who did you come from? What are you made of? It is important to think about and decide on these questions. Your well-being, expression, attitude, productivity, and everything hinges on who you are and how you see yourself.

If you came from the William's family, you will have the DNA, mannerisms and simulations of that family. Simply stated, you get your identity from them. You came from somebody from a certain place. I now live in Stone Mountain, Georgia but I came from North Carolina, from the Ellison family. Let me further prove my point. A whale comes from the ocean from a whale family. It doesn't come from a garden from the cucumber family. You and I know that is ridiculous. Ants don't come from the ocean from the salmon family. That's stupid. Hello, men! Let's wake up, be alert and alive to where we come from.

From the physical dimension, we came from our dad and mom. We are the product of who they are or were. You are also the product of how they thought, dreamed and acted. At least you can change and improve on what they gave you, and you should. You did not come from an ape, monkey or gorilla. I don't care what scientist, book or institution tells you differently. You came from the Creator of all things; The God of the Bible. Period. Nothing else makes sense. God thought of you, designed you, and declared what you are to be like. Do you want proof? Go to Genesis 1:26, *"And God said, let us make man in our image, and after our likeness."* Period!

Our identity, purpose evolution and maturity is rooted in what the Creator said. We weren't created to be stupid, foolish, idiots, and thugs. We were created to be intelligent, wise, productive, rulers. The rest of the above verse proves it. *"...And let them have dominion (rulership) over the fish of the sea, the fowl of the air, and over the cattle, over all the earth and over every creeping thing that creeps upon the earth."* You can't be dumb, stupid and ignorant when you have such responsibilities as this verse describes. So then, our identity is of the God-class. You have his DNA, his make-up. There's intelligence, wit and creativity in you. Love, peace, joy, strength, and might are part of your make-up. You have the ability to do to all the rest of creation what it can't do to you – rule.

To rule, dominate and have authority over everything else in your environment, you must know who you are, whose you are, and why you were purposed. Look no further. All of it is found in what you just read. Read it over and over and over again. Think about it. Grow in it and impart it to others. Think like a ruler; think like someone in charge of and responsible for things. Study people who rule their spheres well. Read books on stewardship and management. Consume all the information you can on leadership.

5

There is plenty of it. Don't be lazy and a procrastinator on this stuff. Your identity depends on it and the world depends on what you bring to the table.

CRISIS #2 – THE HOME ENVIRONMENT

Everything grows from an environment, birds, cattle, sheep, lions, plants and yes – humans. The environment is critical to the nurturance, protection, growth and development of a thing. A home that is dysfunctional, malfunctioning or simply out of alignment with God's intended purpose is also a contributor to the male crisis. Now I realize that there are many great men and women who have evolved without being the in ideal home environment. However, there are many individuals whose lives got grossly off course for lack of a nurturing environment.

When I think about the awesome works of our God, my heart is continuously struck with awe. He spoke galaxies into existence, formed mountains, filled the oceans, and planted forests with a magnificent range of color and variety. But the masterpiece that reveals more about God than anything else shows up where God made the family. The family has two essential elements, marriage and parenthood, that reveals God's character like nothing else he created. The love shown between a husband and wife is invaluable to a child's emotional, psychological, and social development. Without it a child carries a sense of disorientation. Unfortunately, many males and females don't know what it looks like. They never saw it consistently demonstrated. God's intention was that the husband and wife be seen, not merely read about.

Now let's consider the parenting element. This element is critical to every species born into the earth. Its primary purpose is to raise the young to be fully functional adults who can take care of themselves. This is done by feeding, loving, protecting, being with, mentoring, coaching, and guiding the young. Even the animal world knows this. I love studying lions. In all my studies of them, I have never seen a lion cub deliberately abandoned by its parents. I have never seen one given to the elephant family to be taken care of and raised up. Yet, we see scores of young men left to fend for themselves. Many dads are nowhere around. They are not in the picture of that child's life. Then there are those who are there, but aren't properly functioning for whatever reason.

Hey dads, wake up! Get up! Do your God-given role in your children's lives. Every role carries with it responsibilities that are to yield results of empowerment for the next generation. Don't let the animals be wiser and better than us. Create and protect the home environment that builds comfort, confidence, and will power in your children.

CRISIS #3 – MISGUIDED PURPOSE

Let us hear the conclusion of the whole matter: fear God and keep his commandments: for this is the whole duty of man.
Ecclesiastes 12:13

The most important thing to discover in life is the purpose of a thing. Purpose deals with why a thing was created. We understand this when it comes to what man has created. We know that a car wasn't designed to fly. We know that airplanes weren't designed to travel on our highways. We know that the refrigerators were not made to cook in as well as stoves don't freeze food.

Much of male problems come from misguided purpose. We have been led to be someone we were not designed to be. We have been manipulated to operate outside our design and in many cases, we have been abandoned to find or figure out our purpose on our own. Our Creator left nothing to chance. He set a system in place so that every species of beings could learn about their purpose from the preceding species. Again, lion cubs learn from their pride about who they are. Fish learn from those in their school of fish. Baby elephants learn from their parents and so on with every species.

How can we expect to have a society filled with responsible, productive, God-fearing men when there is a lack of men to train the males? Every species has its system intact for developing the young except us as humans – it seems. Now, I realize this is not the case in every place. However, we have too many cases where the man "dropped them and forgot them." You know what I mean. He helped produce the baby, then forgot about the baby and its mother.

So then, where does the young male go to find his purpose, his identity, and how to be a man? Unfortunately, many males go to the grave never knowing their purpose, never becoming fully developed, self-activated men, being the expression of God He intended them to be. The late Dr. Myles Monroe used to say, "The purpose of a thing is found in the mind of the maker. If you want to know your purpose, go to the one who created you. If you think you created yourself then you should ask yourself. If you think the ape created you, then ask the ape. If you think evolution or a big bang created you, then ask them."

Save yourself some time. Don't be that stupid. Stop even trying to find out from "the boys." You know the barber that many men listen to while getting a haircut, the guy on TV who looks like he has it all together or the influential guy in the community who is cheating on his wife? No! Go to God or people who know Him. God has the purpose and plans for your existence (Jeremiah 29:11). As your Creator, He purposed you. He wants you successful. He wants you happy and fulfilled. You were created to be an expression of His greatness. You are His product. No creator designs a product for failure. Every inventor creates a product to represent their name, fulfill a need, and to be an example of possibility.

You were created to represent God (Genesis 1:26). You were created to be a great steward (Genesis 2:15). You were created to be a ruler (Psalm 8:5-8).

MY STORY

I know what it looks like to be raised without a father. I was. It leaves a child with deficits he or she didn't even know they have. In my case, as I look back over the early years, I see where my lack of confidence, lack of aggression and timidity came from. They had their roots in a lack of affirmation. Dad was not there to affirm or bless me.

Many fathers have no clue of the "Power of the Blessing" they have. To bless means to affirm, speak well of or empower to prosper. God did it to Adam and Eve in Genesis 1:28. Jacob did it to his sons in Genesis chapter 49. Jesus did it to his disciples in Matthew chapter 5. It is all throughout the bible. God intended it as a part of parenting, especially from the father. I never got it from my biological father. I don't believe he knew about it.

My father never married my mother; therefore, I was not raised in an environment led by a leader confident of who he was and instilling that confidence in me. Of course, early on I didn't know I needed that and much more. I was merely fighting to survive. I didn't know I needed the image of a real, godly man; psychological development, social skills training, a can-do-attitude and a whole lot of other empowerments that would enable me to be a fully functioning responsible man. I eventually got it, but not from my dad. Fathers, don't let your children go through this. Be there, in the family giving them the love, care, coaching and mentoring they so long desire and desperately need.

The most I would see my father would be during the summer time. I don't recollect seeing him during the year. During the summer visits, he would give me a few dollars and remind me that he was my dad. There were no trips, no movies, no hugs, no blessings, and no "I love you." I believe he never got it himself. You can't give away what you don't have.

The image of him hugging and loving my mother, I never saw it. You see, as the song says, "papa was a rolling stone, wherever he laid his hat was his home." He was a baby producer but not a nurturing father nor a loving husband. The woman he did marry, he gave her pure hell! Don't think I am trying to bash him. That's not my intent. I am merely describing the reality I remember and unfortunately what many children experience today.

I was in my thirties when I found out I had an older brother and younger sisters from my dad (outside the half brothers and sisters he had from the woman he was married to). Such madness must stop. There is no consideration for the devastating affects it has on the children and the tendency of the same actions to be repeated in the next generation. I used to think that my two half-brothers and sisters from my dad's wife had it good. They had a dad and mom in the home. They lived in a much better home that the ones I was raised in and rode in better cars. From my observation of them, I just knew they had everything I dreamed of having as far as a family with a dad, mom, harmony, security, provisions, and etc. was concerned. Boy, was I wrong!

My half-sister (of the marriage) said to me, "Calvin, you were dreaming." She said I was better off than they were without him. She said they and their mother went through chaos. He continuously fussed, cussed and came home when he wanted to.

He abused their mother mentally and physically and neglected them as children. His mother (their grandmother) had to repeatedly get on him to buy clothes for them and provide for his family. To my amazement she said that our father's brothers treated their wives and children the same way. The Bible says that the sons of the fathers would affect their children to the third and fourth generations (Exodus 34:7). I can only wonder what was imparted into my father and his brothers. I don't know. He never shared such information with me. We never sat and talked like that.

He made my half-brothers so mad that they greatly resented him. One of them refused to go to his funeral. He never imparted to us the images and legacy of a husband's love, father-craft and how to honor God with everything placed under his stewardship. If you are a man reading this book with the mentality and behaviors of my father, stop it. Get your heart and life in alignment with God. Let His purpose and kingdom rule your living. After all, He created you. You are on earth to serve His pleasure. Then go to your wife and children and repent of how you have been treating them. Do it before you finish reading this book. Get help. Talk to other God-ruled men. By any means necessary, fix your mess-ups.

Well, things didn't end in a bad state with my dad, at least as far as my half-sister and I was concerned. We went to our father and talked to him. We let him know that how he treated us was painful, but he was forgiven. We would go to his house on several occasions to chat and laugh with him. Of course he would cry and showed remorse over his actions. We felt so good about the ending when he died at age 61.

To this very day, I praise God for enabling me to forgive my father. He will do the same for you. I was determined that with God's help, I would not do my wife and children the way my father did his. Well, as of the date of this book, I have been married to my girlfriend (wife) for over 36 years. One of my greatest rewards is when I get texts or phone calls from my sons saying, "I love you, Dad."

Though I didn't get my father's blessing, because I believe he was unaware that he could do such a thing, I received God's. When I didn't know who my father was, at a young age, God told me He was my Father. Father means source. So God is the one who enabled me to come through the loins of my biological father. So it is with you. If you will embrace this, regardless of your beginnings and even your present state, God will navigate you into the purpose and plans He has for your life (Jeremiah 29:11). It is in God's will that you will find true fulfillment. Like most people, I haven't had a smooth life, but God has blessed me with a great marriage, allowed me to travel to various nations, write several books, develop relationships with a lot of people, and most of all, find fulfillment through pleasing Him.

~Dedication~

Jerard Rhodes, Brockston, MA

Calvin Deon Ellison, Jr., Greenville, NC

De-Andre Smith, Winterville, NC

Daquan Rogers, Winterville, NC

Joshua Rolle, Congers, GA

Brian Walker Jr., Conyers, GA

Justin Knight, Greenville, NC

Jonathan Knight, Greenville, NC

Monte'ell Ellison, Farmville, NC

Caleb Woods, Petersburg, VA

Hermon Woods II, Orlando, FL

Darion Jones, Greensboro, NC

Elijah Rogers, Greenville, NC

Hahceem Rogers, Greenville, NC

Garbriel Elliot, Wilson, NC

Biography of Augustus Corbett, Esquire

Augustus Corbett, Esq. is a pastor, church planter, attorney, author, activist, and blogger. He has been in ministry for over thirty years and a practicing attorney for twelve years. He is passionate about taking the Kingdom of God to the inner city through an apostolic mandate of preaching Jesus, promoting jobs and pursuing justice.

He founded Augustus Corbett Ministries, Impart Publishing, Corbett Law Firm, Saltmakers Church, National Black Parents Association and Texas Urban Renewal Network. He has a Bachelor of Science degree in chemistry from North Carolina Agricultural and Technical State University and a Juris Doctorate from North Carolina Central University School of Law.

Pastor Corbett has preached at many conferences, crusades, revivals, and seminars around the world including the African and European continents. Additionally, he served the nation in the U.S. Navy. As a practicing attorney, he has represented many people in court. He loves seeking justice for his clients. His motto is "Augustus Gets Justice!" He authored the book, ***Education Injustice,*** and has plans of releasing several more books this year including ***Jesus Follower*** and ***Supernatural Soul Winning***.

15

Living in the Dallas, Texas area, his favorite sports teams are the Pittsburgh Steelers, Dallas Mavericks, Texas Rangers, Georgetown Hoyas, and Duke Blue Devils. He enjoys reading, writing, golfing, fishing, hunting, seafood, and catching a great action or thriller movie with his wife.

Pastor Corbett has been happily married to his life partner, Toni, for over thirty years. They have two children Attorney Chloe Corbett, who practices law with him, and Caleb Corbett, a financial analyst in Dallas.

Personal Profile

Key Words

Success, Justice, Discipleship and Kingdom of God

Favorite Quote

"What profit is there to gain the whole world and lose eternal life?"

Values

Integrity, Innovation and Industry

Marketable Skills

Writing, Speaking, Thinking and Leading

Contact Information

Augustus Corbett
Corbett & Corbett LLP
1910 Pacific Ave., Suite 6075
Dallas, TX 75201

Office: (469) 726-2626
Fax: (469) 726-2526
Email: acorbett@corbettfirm.com

REPAIRING BROKEN AFRICAN AMERICAN MEN

Taking the Kingdom of God to Broken African American Men by Preaching Jesus, Promoting Jobs and Pursuing Justice

Augustus Corbett, Esq.

It has been my sincere desire since childhood to empower African American men. This desire entered my heart from witnessing white supremacy oppress African American men severely in my rural southeastern North Carolina hometown. Most African American men in my neighborhood served their white male counterparts although our nation ended slavery decades earlier.

Injustice and inequality were everywhere in the sixties and seventies in my neighborhood. I hated it deeply. I now realize that God gave me this deep hatred for racial injustice. Nevertheless, my deep hatred for racial injustice caused me to reject Jesus and embrace Islam despite growing up in church and knowing God had

17

called me into Christian ministry. I was angry and rebellious. Hence, I dropped out of high school and sold drugs heavily.

Eventually, I moved to New York City, where a neighbor introduced me to the five-percenter religion. This religion is a branch of the Nation of Islam that started inside prisons in the northeast and became very popular with young African American men on the East Coast. My attraction to Islam also occurred because Malcolm X and Black Muslims opposed white supremacy militantly unlike Rev. Dr. Martin Luther King Jr. and his adherents who fought it nonviolently. King's nonviolent approach turned me off, as it seemed to placate and pacify white Americans. I wanted to oppose white supremacy militantly as Malcolm X and the Black Panther Party espoused rather than turn the other cheek as Dr. King advocated.

Fortunately, and thankfully Jesus never gave up on me during this period. He continued to love and watch over me. His steadfast and unconditional love caused me to renounce Islam, return to my Christian roots, and become His committed follower. That was October 1985.

Early in my discipleship process, Jesus forbade me from focusing on the race issue. He wanted me to focus on Him exclusively so I could become a strong disciple. Delving into the racial injustice issues would have distracted me from His discipleship goals.

The Lord released me to revisit racial injustice after a few years. This time, however, love, knowledge, and justice motivated me. My hatred of white supremacy had not abated, but God had taught me how to love and pity white racists, not hate them.

<u>Two Devastating Deaths</u>

My calling to reach African American men crystallized during the height of the crack epidemic in the 80s and 90s after my two youngest brothers were killed, approximately six years apart. Nothing prepared me for their deaths. In fact, I grew up with four brothers and they all died prematurely. God has spared me from the curse that has plagued my family. He spared me because I returned to Christ just in time. Preaching my brothers' funerals was the most challenging thing I have ever done. Their deaths were devastating and convinced me that young African American men were facing an unprecedented crisis that neither America nor I could continue to ignore.

I quickly learned that addressing this crisis is a daunting proposition. White men have designed the entire American system to undermine the development and progress of African American men. From the founding of the country to the present, white men have lynched, murdered, and savagely oppressed millions of African American men including recent incidents of appalling police brutality. Even worse is the self-hatred that African American men have learned from white supremacy, being the reason that homicide is the leading cause of death for African American men. The Centers For Disease Control reports that the homicide rate for African-Americans quadruples the national average.[1]

My heart is crushed as I witness poverty, joblessness, failing schools, mass incarceration, and early death devour an entire generation of young African American men. Years ago, I sought the Lord in despair about reaching young African American men.

---

[1] https://www.acsh.org/news/2017/08/10/african-american-homicide-rate-nearly-quadruple-national-average-11680

He gave me the answer — He said, *"Take them my Kingdom."* His powerful words became my mandate.

My understanding of the Kingdom of God was minimal initially, especially how it could transform the lives of young African American men. It took many years of prayer, research, and Bible study for the Lord to teach me that taking the Kingdom of God to African American men practically could be accomplished by *preaching Jesus, promoting Jobs, and pursuing Justice*. I explain below how taking the Kingdom of God to African American men equals taking them *Jesus, Jobs, and Justice*.

<u>Preaching Jesus</u>

Life for all humans, including African American men, begins with Jesus. He came to earth so that we could have the abundant life. In John 10:10, He's King of the Kingdom. The Bible says His throne will last forever.

Taking the Kingdom of God to African American men begins with a personal relationship with Jesus through the new birth. Once African American men experience the new birth, they become Kingdom citizens, possessing all the benefits of full citizenship.

Becoming Kingdom citizens is only the first step. The next step is intensive discipleship; something I coined *Transformation 360*. The primary focus of *Transformation 360* is to help African American men commit to righteousness, holiness, godliness and other Christian virtues that foster success and achievement. It involves teaching and training African American men Kingdom principles, which cause prosperity and Kingdom living.

Kingdom living uses Kingdom principles to live in victory over the curse. Adam's disobedience activated the curse, and it (the curse) includes all the evil in the world such as white supremacy, fatherlessness, poverty, disease, substance abuse, despair, and so forth. Kingdom living, however, supersedes the curse and produces success and transgenerational prosperity, which can pass from generation to generation. Moreover, Kingdom living protects African American men from premature death.

Satan doesn't want African American men experiencing Kingdom living because of all its benefits. He cleverly alienates many African American men from Jesus with baseless lies and the hypocrisy of some white theologians. Let me explain. As white slaveholders built the slave system and profited from free slave labor, some white theologians and ministers justified slavery by twisting Scriptures. They misused certain Scriptures in the Bible to make the slaves accepting of slavery. This hypocritical perversion of Scripture caused and continue to cause many African American men to distrust Jesus and erect mental walls against biblical knowledge.

Satan also alienates many African American men from Jesus by using the arts to depict Jesus falsely as white. The historical records are clear: neither Jesus nor His disciples were white. They were Hebrews from the Middle East; people of color undoubtedly, perhaps even Black Africans.

This false depiction of Jesus continues to alienate many young African American men from Jesus. We are reversing this alienation by planting a church that accurately depicts Jesus as a man of color, a man who is relatable and relevant to issues facing African American men. One such issue that Jesus is concerned about for African American men is the critically high unemployment and joblessness of African American men.

Promoting Jobs

Jesus is not aloof from and indifferent to the needs of African American men. He knows their desperate need for jobs, careers, fair wages, and so on. Despite the low unemployment rate generally, Jesus knows the unemployment rate for African American men continues to be at least two times higher than for white men.[2] The unemployment rate for young African American men is over 50% in some cities, such as Chicago. This percentage is staggering, and it shows how deeply entrenched racism is in America. Unemployment is so dire for many African American men they have quit looking for work and vanished from unemployment records. This high level of unemployment and joblessness contributes to the concentrated poverty and crime in many African American neighborhoods.

African American men desperately need jobs for another significant reason. Like all men, African American men find their identity in their jobs and careers. God placed in the DNA of all men the desire to work and provide for their families. The self-worth of men, African American men included, primarily emanates from the ability of men to provide for their families. Without jobs, African American men cannot provide for their families and thus feel worthless and hopeless. Many unemployed African American men commit crimes to feed themselves, which further exacerbates their inability to find jobs because crime produces felony records.

Our nonprofit, the Texas Urban Renewal Network (TURN), has developed several initiatives to address African American male unemployment. One program we developed is the Creating Economic Opportunities for Yourself or the CEO program. The

---

[2] https://www.bls.gov/web/empsit/cpsee_e16.htm

goal of this program is teaching African American men with criminal records how to start businesses, become entrepreneurs, and be their own CEOs. We desire to rebuild the economic base in the African American community that we abandoned started in the 1960s following desegregation.

Furthermore, God can solve unemployment and joblessness for African American men if they seek first His Kingdom and righteousness. God promises to cause African American men to thrive if they turn to Him. He will draw corporate investments and cause the entrepreneur spirit to abound in African American men when they learn to apply Kingdom principles to their lives. He will supernaturally provide jobs and cause their careers and business endeavors to prosper. He will rebuke the devourer and cause poverty to stand down. The nation will marvel as God transforms African American men economically and empower them to create wealth. As He caused Israel to prosper, He will do the same for African American men if they trust and put Him first.

Pursuing Justice

The concept of justice is not secular and did not originate with humans. It originated with God. It's as much a part of God's character as holiness, faith, love, and truth. According to Psalm 89:14, the very throne of God comprises justice and righteousness, and the Prophet Amos instructed Israel to let *"justice roll down like waters and righteousness like an ever-flowing stream"* (Amos 5:24).

The Hebrew word for justice is *mishpat*. In his book, *Generous Justice*, Dr. Timothy Keller, Pastor of Redeemer Presbyterian Church in New York defines justice as protecting the rights of the vulnerable. His definition of justice demonstrates the importance of justice in a fallen world where the powerful often devour the weak. His description reminds us that without justice, the rights of the vulnerable would be swept away by the powerful. His definition also teaches us that justice demands that society enacts laws that prevent and punish unjust exploitation of the weak and promote equitable opportunities for the vulnerable.

Many of our white evangelical brethren have a difficult time embracing God's demand and prescriptions for justice because historically they have practiced extreme injustice toward African Americans. They constructed a legal system that brutally enslaved and stripped African Americans of dignity and humanity. Only after Jesus moved white Christian abolitionists to demand justice for enslaved African Americans were white plantation owners forced to dismantle slavery vis-à-vis a horrific Civil War.

White plantation owners were still unbowed and stubborn even after the Civil War. They refused to show justice to its newly freed African American citizens and instead enacted Jim Crow laws to segregate and oppress them. This awful Jim Crow system lasted another hundred years. However, God is just, and once again, He used the church via the civil rights movement to demand justice for vulnerable, African Americans.

History proves that from ancient Israel to modern day America the Lord has consistently been on the side of the vulnerable. He has opposed injustice since He created humans. Even today, He is forcing America to create a more just society for all Americans. Hence, we thank God for the progress America has experienced in social, political and economic justice, culminating in the election and re-election of the first African American President. Notwithstanding Barack Obama's election and re-election, there is still lots of work before America can be a just and great nation.

My motto is to celebrate the progress but continue the protest because America's stubborn progress in racial, political and

24

economic justice is not complete nor guaranteed. We can never rest in our fight for justice because some of our deeply conservative white evangelical brethren fear the changing demographics of America. They are determined to "take America back" through such tactics as mass incarceration, voter suppression, and attacks on affirmative action.

The fight for justice additionally demands the destruction of systemic and institutionalized racism. The great institutions of America are ripe with systemic racial injustice. For example, the education system unjustly traps many young African American men in failing schools, kicking them out, or placing them in special education disproportionately. I invite you to read my book *Education Injustice* to learn more about how the failing public education system marginalizes African American males.

As an attorney, I have witnessed how the criminal justice system unjustly imprisons many young nonviolent African American men and leave them disenfranchised and marginalized. The health care system unjustly denies many young vulnerable African American men equal health care. The corporate system unjustly denies young vulnerable African American men equal job and career opportunities.

These are only several examples of the continual systemic racial injustice plaguing America. As committed Christians, we must do as early Christians did throughout American history: we must preach, teach and demonstrate the love and Kingdom of God by demanding justice for these young vulnerable African American men. As Christ followers, we must follow the example of Jesus and His true and faithful followers throughout history who refused to stand by and remain silent as injustice and inequality prevailed.

<u>Conclusion</u>

The issues confronting African American men are deeply entrenched but not insurmountable. Our nation can solve these issues. It is my firm belief that efforts like those I outlined below will empower African American men to better themselves, their families/children and the African American community at large. They require a concerted effort by churches, businesses, and other stakeholders in the black community. Here are my suggestions:

1. Adopt measures to stop the violence and self-hatred

2. Focus African American churches on evangelization and discipleship for African American men

3. Recruit and train strong African American men to mentor struggling African American men

4. Reconnect African American men to their families

5. Replace dependency thinking with the self-reliant mindset

6. Get African American men job ready

7. Foster the entrepreneur spirit

8. Reform and adequately fund the public education system, including charter schools

9. Reform the criminal justice system

10. Reform the child support system

~Dedication~

I dedicate my contribution to this work to my
five deceased brothers:

†Bill Corbett

†Anthony Young

†Adolf James

†Leon James

†Mike Corbett

Biography of Apostle Alvin Deal

Apostle Alvin Deal is a ministerial visionary, empowering leader, extraordinary teacher, entrepreneur, spiritual director, community humanitarian, devoted husband and father, and a trailblazer on various platforms. Alvin Deal, a native of Greenwood, South Carolina, was called to preach God's word at the age of 22. He was called to pastor his first church at age 23. The anointed Words of God took Pastor Deal's ministry from level to level. He has pastored five Baptist churches and founded three non-denominational churches. He is the Founder and Senior Pastor of the Faith Christian Center Church, a thriving ministry that is dedicated to preaching and teaching the Word of God in a practical and uncompromising manner who faithfully, passionately and is diligently dedicated to building a people of purpose, power and praise. He is a man of solid integrity whose countless contributions to over 36 years of ministry has touched and impacted the lives of many.

Apostle Deal is married to the love of his life, Lady Georgia Deal and together they forge forward, ministering with simplicity God's plan and purpose for His people. They have three children Fauwnia, Isaiah and Aukeem and five grandchildren Ja'arious, Rezavious, Timothy, Tierra and Kasen, Dre, Johnathan, Aniyah, Cruz and Omari.

Apostle Deal is a community activist that is deeply involved in his community in so many different ways. He travels the state and

29

country providing workshop, seminars, and presentations for schools, businesses, community groups and other organizations. He is a highly sought after motivational presenter that gets his message across with a bang.

Apostle Deal has served in many different capacities in the community such as:

- Greenwood Chamber of Commerce Board Member
- Lander Foundation Board Member
- Piedmont Technical College Foundation Board Member
- PALS Chairperson
- Coordinator of Project GANG.
- Black Male Conference Presenter, Benedict College
- Faith Works Initiative Department Of Alcohol Drug Abuse Services (DOADAS)
- National Black Family Summit Presenter

Apostle Deal's philosophy is that there are three kinds of people in the world:

1. Those that LET things happen
2. Those that DONT CARE what happens
3. AND THOSE THAT MAKE THINGS HAPPEN!

Apostle Deal makes it happen daily, walking by faith, not by sight!

Personal Profile

Key Words
Bold, Courageous, Pioneer, Visionary, Strong, Faithful, Solid, Innovative

Favorite Quotes
- "What you make happen for others will happen for you. "
- "Buy the Truth and Sell it NOT."
- "What did God say?"

Values
Bridge Builder, Trustworthy, Visionary, Healthy Relationships

Marketable Skills
Public Speaking, Organizer, Leadership abilities,, Networking skills, Continued Learning techniques

Contact Information
Email: Alvin_deal@yahoo.com
Website: www.alvindealministries.org
Facebook: Apostle Alvin Deal

FREE TO BECOME

Apostle Alvin Deal

I f we would look back over our lives, we might find many mistakes and missteps on our journey of life. Somewhere way back in the early years of our growth and development, when we were ten feet tall and bullet proof, the world was waiting on us to conquer it and we grabbed it by the tail and off we went not knowing the pitfalls that awaited us. No one could tell us anything because we were grown. I remember that time just like it was yesterday; I had just graduated from high school. My mind was set on being the best man that Greenwood High School had ever produced. I had something to prove to myself, my family, and my friends. Many of my classmates went to college; some went to the military. Others like me set off on the course to be successful, by any means necessary.

In my city, there were many textile factories that provided job opportunities. Since I was already employed at the time of my graduation, I wanted more. So I set out on this journey to become a prosperous man. Being a young black male from the country, I had a desire to see the world and to make something out of myself. I

32

only had my high school diploma, dreams of making it big, and one of my prized possessions: a 1972 blue and white half vainer top 442 Oldsmobile Cutlass Supreme. I had just purchased it and it was spectacular. I remember saying to myself I'm going to get the girls now. I had owned a few old clunkers before but this car was in a category all by itself.

While driving down one of the main streets of Greenwood with my windows down, the car washed and shining real clean, I noticed that people were waving at me and even some of the pretty ladies had smiles on their faces. Many of them I knew and some I didn't. It really did not matter; I felt like a big important man while riding in my new car. My friend that was riding with me quickly brought me back to reality. He said, "Al, they are not waving or smiling at you but they are waving and smiling at your new car."

I tried to convince him that he was wrong and that I was the reason for all that wonderful attention. How could they not notice me? I am a high school graduate with a new car and I am good looking. But deep down on the inside, I knew he was right, but it really did make me feel good thinking that someone might be looking at me like I was a man of success. I dropped my friend off at his home, pushed my eight track tape player in my Cutlass and began to listen to the sounds of soul as I made my way home. That night I made up my mind that I was going to accept the invitation that I had gotten from my girlfriend and grandmother to come stay with them in Orlando, Florida. Mind you, I had never driven outside of the state of South Carolina, and in order to get to Florida, we had to drive on the interstate highway. If this is what it took to prove that I was a man, so be it. I made plans to move to Orlando, Florida.

I only had a small amount of cash from my job that I had saved up. My mom advised me to make sure that I had a job waiting on me when I got there. That was her way of making sure that her son would not be a burden to anyone and if I did not secure a job, I really didn't need to quit my present job to go on this wild goose chase. That is what she said with crystal clarity. I thought to myself I am grown. I will do what I want to do and that's that. But you know like I knew back then, you dare not voice your thoughts unless you wanted some swift correction. I mean hands on correction that changed your thought patterns many times immediately. Because I wanted to prove to myself and to others that I was a responsible young adult, well able to make grown up decisions without the helpful hands of my parents, I called my girlfriend's grandfather and I easily convinced him to get me a job where he worked. He assured me that I had a job upon my arrival in Florida. Then it was settled; I could start my journey into manhood without the restraints of parental oversight in a major vacation destination for millions of people. I was so very excited about this awesome adventure in which I believed would be a starting point for me as a young man. I had no idea how my life was about to change, because I was not prepared for this world that I wanted to conquer. I had it by the tail and I was about to feel its kick.

Many thoughts of great expectation and anticipation kept me on such a high that was unexplainable. We mapped out our trip on what roads to take trying very hard to avoid the interstate. I plotted out a course that took us through the state of Georgia without having to drive on the interstate until we got into Jacksonville, Florida. From there, it was as easy as pie. I wondered why I never ventured out like that before. It was breathtaking driving at such a high rate of speed and to think, it was all legal.

We arrived at her grandmother's house on a beautiful June afternoon. The weather was perfect. As I checked out the view, I noticed several orange trees in the front yard and many others throughout the neighborhood. We unpacked and got settled in our new residence. Everything was going well for the first couple of days. The weekend was over and now it was work time, so I asked about my job that would be awaiting me upon my arrival. Now, here is the curve ball that life will throw at you when you are not prepared. He told me that he was still *working* on it and to be patient. I didn't know what patient was at the time. I said to him, "You promised me a job and I left a good job, making good money and I expected to go right to work." Well, several weeks went by, but there was still no job. The little money that I had was gone and now I was at the mercy of people I just barely knew. I was very disappointed to say the least. It seemed like my incredible dreams were quickly turning into a nightmare. All kind of thoughts were going through my mind; thoughts like *how are you going to take care of the baby that's on the way? What will people think of you now?* No job, no money; seemly no hope in sight. Day after day and there was no good news. Then finally late one Friday evening, I was on the front porch wondering what I should do when her grandfather pulled up in the yard with a big smile on his face. He got out of the car and came directly over to me and said, "You got the job and they want you to start work on Monday morning!"

I thanked him and said, "I will be there." Later that day he drove me out to the plant where he worked to show me how to get there. The plant was closed but that was alright with me because I was again excited about having an opportunity to prove to everybody that I was a man.

I got in my car that Monday morning and started on my way to work. I actually got there before many of the other workers. After many weeks of much hard labor, I made friends with many of the guys that I worked with. Let me tell you a little bit about the work we were doing. I ran what we would call today a jack hammer. We worked with cement molds building window seals and door headers for homes and business. The company was a multimillion dollar operation and I had ambitions of climbing to the top while working here. The weeks grew into months and the work never stopped. It was hard work and long hours and the only thing I got was not a promotion but calluses on both my hands from operating the jack hammer without wearing gloves. Many of the guys that I worked with didn't have their own transportation, so I was able to provide transportation for them for a fee. Since I had this fancy 1972 442 Oldsmobile Cutlass, it was an offer they could not refuse. I only charged eleven dollars per person. I was getting paid twice on pay day, once from my job and from my riders. The money was coming in and I was on my way to becoming a "man."

But there was one thing that I failed to mention and it was that I was a compulsive gambler. It was a habit that I picked up from my brothers and my cousins. We all gambled; it was a way of life for us. It did not seem like it was nothing wrong because we did it for fun, we did it for pleasure and for recreation. But now I was making this money and I felt the urge to go to the gambling house where I spent most of my time trying to win and hit it big. Drinking and smoking with people I barely knew. This went on week after week until I did not have money for gas, food for lunch; however, because I had made many friends on the job, they shared their lunches with me. On the other hand, one of my foreign friends would share oatmeal cookies and tell me to drink some water. Oatmeal cookies would make me thirsty and the water would make me full, but after doing that for a period of weeks, I developed stomach pains. By now you can recognize that I am struggling to become the man that I hoped or dreamt to become.

One day I was given an opportunity to make some extra money for gas by giving my foreign friend a ride to downtown Orlando to see a special lady who he called "Mummie." I was not sure about the relationship, but I needed the money. Upon arriving at her home, he invited me in the house with him. When we entered the house, he greeted her with smiles and hugs. It was evident that he had visited her before. She was sitting in a chair with a Bible in her lap. My friend said to her, "Mummie give me numbers." She wrote some numbers on a paper and she gave them to him. He in turn gave her an undisclosed amount of money. He then introduced me as his friend "Jitterbug" known as "Jit" on the job. He told her that I was having problems with my stomach. She beckoned me closer to her and the strangest thing happened. She put her hands on my stomach, told me my first girlfriend's name from junior high school and said that I would be alright. Then she looked at me with a glare of expectation and I told her thank you and we left. I had gotten my money from my foreign friend for taking him and that was all that I had. We left the house and as were entered the car, she came out of the house and sat on the porch. I turn the ignition to start the car, but the car for the first time since I purchased it would not start. This was strange because the car had never given me any problems before. We tried and we tried. We checked the battery and everything. We were there for forty-five minutes. We went up the street to street to another coworker who was a master mechanic. He checked out the car and found no problems. After an hour and half of trouble shooting when we were about to give up, I noticed that the lady called Mummie got up out of her chair on the porch and went in the house. As soon as she went in the house, the car started. The car drove fine and we made it back home.

That night, I had a strange dream that my car had been in an accident. It was so real that I got up the next morning to check for damages. To my surprise, there was no damage, but the dream was so real. So I got dressed for work and when I arrived, I pulled between two cars. I went to my work station and the two coworkers whose cars I parked between were already there. When we took a break for lunch, everyone went to the warehouse to eat their lunch. I was the only one that went to the parking lot and no one else went outside of the gate before me. When I got in the car and sat down for a while, I had this feeling to check my car because I still remembered the dream. I got out of the car, checked and there was tremendous damage to the passenger side door of my Cutlass Supreme! It was the strangest thing because I was the last to pull in the parking lot and the first to go to the parking lot. It was as if the car was damaged by a supernatural force, because it was unexplainable. The drivers of the two cars never left the building!

After that day, the car would crank when it wanted to. Eventually, I had no more use for the car. I began to drink, smoke and gamble every chance I could get. With no money coming into the household from me, I was asked to carry my part of the bills. I became angry and violent to the point that my girlfriend's grandparents were afraid of me. I woke up one morning with a strong desire to go to church though I had never been to church since I arrived in Florida. I got in the car and to my surprise, it started that morning. I drove around the neighborhood, looking at what church I would attend. Finally, I saw one; the parking lot was filled with cars. I found a parking space and I made my way inside. I must have gotten there during the announcements. I sat there for fifteen to twenty minutes and I got up and left. I drove back home and sat in the car listening to gospel music for about an hour and half, then the feeling just left. I called my brother and told him all about the car and that he could come and get the car. Before they came and got the car, I made one last attempt to drive it but it only cranked when it wanted to. So my decision was final; come get it.

This entire event was very puzzling to me and the downward spiral began. The car was gone. Then I got in an argument with the supervisor and he eventually fired me. After getting fired from the job, I had no money coming in and my girlfriend left me and went back to South Carolina. I was put out of the house of her grandparents and I ended up getting a room at a boarding house in downtown Orlando in the red light district. At this point of my journey, I was lost and on my own, at least that is what I thought. Hungry, broke, and disappointed, my dreams of becoming this self-made superman was gone and going back to my hometown in that situation was unthinkable. I didn't have a relationship with the Lord at that time, but I had heard someone say if you call on Him, He would answer prayer. I did not know where to begin, so I just said, "Help me, Lord; please help me!"

The next day, one of my old friends from the neighborhood where my girlfriend's grandparents lived, contacted me. He said he needed some help picking oranges. I went with him and I made enough money to pay my room rent for a couple of days. When that money was gone, I got with some Haitian fruit pickers that lived in the boarding house. That day early in the morning while I was working so hard, I said to myself, "Shame or no shame; I am going home!" I made enough money to buy a bus ticket back to Greenwood, South Carolina. The ticket only cost $37.23 cents one way. Working in the orange grove that day I had made forty-five dollars. When I got back to my room, I got involved in a gambling game and I lost my bus ticket money. I was thinking this would be a good chance for me to have some money in my pocket when got back to town. But, it didn't work out as I planned. Now I had no bus fare, no food and no rent money for my room. The only thing that I had was an expensive keepsake watch that I had been holding onto. I did the unthinkable. I sold it for way less than what it was valued. I only got enough to purchase my bus ticket. I got on that bus headed back to Greenwood, South Carolina with no car, no girlfriend, no money, no dreams and my life totally out of control. Not only that, but my clothes were dirty; the few pieces that I still had left. Remember, I wanted to be "Free to be a Man."

Now, I was free from school. I was free from my parents. I was free from what I called my limiting community in which I grew up and I was free to be whoever and whatever I wanted to be. Now, I was really free. I was at the bottom of life now with less than what I started with. But there was something happening to me that I could not explain. Weird dreams and nightmares that I would wake up from in my sleep feeling scared and my heart beating a hundred times faster than normal. There were times that I would wake up unable to move or speak. It was terrifying. Who could I tell about this? No one would believe a pothead. The dreams became more and more frequent. I remember being surrounded by millions of snakes in one dream and in another dream I was being chased by huge monsters and yet another dream, I would be falling in a very dark bottomless pit that never seemed to end. I often wondered what was going on with me.

Before going to Florida, I never had such dreams or any of those strange happenings even when I had been smoking weed and drinking. During that time, I didn't really want to go to many places, so I stayed at home because I was ashamed that I had failed. One Sunday morning, I was invited to go to church by my brother who had just given his life to Christ a few months earlier. I said to myself, "*Maybe I can at least find me a new girlfriend there.*" I agreed to go to church with him and when I got there, it was like nothing I have ever seen in my life. The music was loud and people were dancing in the church. Then after all of that, the preacher preached for a whole hour and a half. It seemed to me he was talking about me all through his sermon saying, "You been smoking dope; you been gambling and midnight rambling; you been drinking liquor and committing fornication!" He kept saying, "You been in and out of the night clubs!"

Now you know I am a mad somebody right about now! But then he said something that forever changed my life. He said, "God will forgive you and help you become the man that you have always wanted to be." That day, I gave my life to Christ. It was only the beginning of my journey to real freedom. After being a believer for many years, there were still unanswered questions about the dreams and those unexplainable things that were still happening to me. They were not as frequent as they were before I got saved, but they were just as real. I wanted answers so I prayed and asked for help from the God of the Bible. One day I was in my work truck with my radio on the Christian station, where there were different preachers on during the day. I heard a minister say in his message that if you have had your palm read, or if you have played with an Ouija board or if you participated in the occult in some form or another, you have opened yourself up to demonic activity. I pulled my truck over to the side of the road and began to listen very intently. He described some of the same things that I was experiencing in my dreams and even while awake. I listened to him as he gave instructions on how to be free from this power of darkness. The pastor said if you have been involved in those activities you have opened a door for the enemy to attack you whenever he pleases because the door had never been closed; even if you are a Christian. The only way to freedom from those attacks was you had to repent of it, renounce it, reject it, ask for forgiveness, and walk away from it, in Jesus' Name. Let me tell you something. Right there on the side of the road in my work truck, I followed those instructions to the letter. From that day to this one, I have never had any more of those dreams, nightmares, or unexplainable situations ever again.

Now I know the only real freedom that I have is in Christ Jesus. I have the power now to be *Free To Become* whoever God has called me to be. A Jewish carpenter once said to them that believe on Him, to them He would give them power to become the sons of God!

~Dedication~

To the young men that I have released upon the earth, my sons, Isaiah and Aukeem and my grandsons Ja'arious, Rezavious, Dre, Timothy, Johnathan, Harlan and Omari:

As I watch you face the challenges of life, I want you to be prepared for what lies ahead. Your determination in life inspired me to dedicate this chapter to you. So that you will not fall into the pitfalls that I encountered on life's journey, knowing always that you are free to become all that God has destined you to be. There will be no curses that can hold you down and no generational bondages that will bind you, because of the blood of Jesus Christ for whom the son makes free is free indeed. (John 8:32)

For if the blood of bulls and goats, and the ashes of an heifer sprinkling the unclean, sanctifieth to the purifying of the flesh; how much more shall the blood of Christ, who through the eternal Spirit offered himself without spot to God, purge your conscience from dead works to serve the living God? (Hebrews 9:13-14)

Walk and live in the freedom that has been bought and paid for on your behalf. May this chapter of my life help you to see that you have everything life has to offer when you are in a relationship with Him!

Biography of Pastor Vernon W. Durand

Pastor Vernon W. Durand is the current Pastor of Community Christian Ministries located in Lithonia, Georgia, which he started in 2011. Before pastoring at Community Christian Ministries, Pastor Durand cofounded Love Tabernacle International Fellowship in Brooklyn, New York where he served as Assistant Pastor for about 11 years. As Assistant Pastor, he also served as Music and Worship Director, Youth Leader, and Sunday School Superintendent.

He has been a part of several gospel bands both in his native Dominica and in Brooklyn, New York, including The Gospel Proclaimers, Heaven's Children, Direct Messengers and Essence of Love of which he served as band leader.

Pastor Durand has also served as a Radio Host on WKDM Radio in New York City where he hosted a gospel show featuring American and Caribbean Gospel music and preaching of the Word of God. He also made appearance on Brooklyn's local television network, B-Cat, introducing and ending a local community program.

Most recently, he served as a police officer with the DeKalb County Police Department where he served with honor for 10 years. He obtained his Bachelor's degree in Biblical Studies and Ministry at Texas-based, Nation 2 Nation Christian University. He's been married to his wife Miriam for 36 years and together they have four children and four grandchildren.

Personal Profile

Key Words

Embrace, Learn, Painful, Succeed

Favorite Quote

"Knowledge plus courage equal success." Pastor Durand

Marketable Skills

Youth Development, Preaching, Mentoring, Counseling

Contact Information

Email: Pastordccm@gmail.com

Website: www.ccmgeorgia.org

Phone: 404.545.5595

BECOMING A MAN

Pastor Vernon W. Durand

I f you took a moment to read my biography, you would have already obtained a little bit of information about me; nevertheless, please allow me to share a little more about myself with you. I am married and have been to the same gorgeous wife, Miriam for the past 36 years, a union that has produced three sons and one beautiful daughter. I am also very proud to have been blessed with three lovely granddaughters and one grandson. I currently serve as Pastor of Community Christian Ministries located at1693 S. Deshon Road in Lithonia, Georgia.

I was born on the Caribbean Island of Dominica and it was there that I had my personal encounter with the Lord Jesus Christ and accepted Him as my Lord and Savior at a very tender age of 14 years and was baptized at the age of 16 years old. Since then, I have been actively involved in ministry up to this present time.

I migrated to New York City, United States in the late 1980s, where I have continued to serve in many different areas of ministry, including Youth Director, Sunday School

Superintendent, and Music and Worship leader, in a church that I co-founded.

After living in New York City for about 22 years, the Lord spoke through my dear wife in reference to moving to Georgia. That we did in 2007 at the direction of the Holy Spirit but without any clear directive as to the reason for the move. Upon moving to Georgia, I had absolutely no intent of further involvement in ministry other than to serve under the authority or pastoral care of another. That I did for approximately three and a half years until the voice of the Lord came roaring like thunder, and made it abundantly clear what He had brought us to Georgia for. We were to get started in ministry again, hence the birth of Community Christian Ministries.

God has indeed blessed us Community Christian Ministries with a very fine group of believers for whom I thank Him every day. CCM, as we affectionately call ourselves, is a closely-knit church family where love abounds. It is not only talked about but also exercised, practiced and demonstrated in the true sense and spirit of the word. Finally, a church you can call your own.

Besides serving on the battlefield for the Lord, I am also very proud to have served with the DeKalb County Georgia Police department for 10 years. That experience has helped to equip me in many ways, to deal with the many demons that plague my community, especially those affecting our young black men, many of whom have in some way, become targets of law enforcement across the United States.

In this chapter, *"Becoming a Man,"* it is my hope to provide you the reader with some valuable tools helpful to the art of raising a son and preparing for manhood.

<u>The Painful Reality</u>

It is a very sad reality that our young men are being incarcerated on a much higher rate than any other race in our society. A 2013 census survey showed that the United States represents 4.4 percent of the world's population, yet housed 22 percent of the world's prisoners. According to that survey, male blacks accounted for 37 percent of that total.

There has been many theories as to the reason this occurs; some of which makes sense and others leave quite a bit of room for questioning and reasoning. However, if we are to understand the real reason behind the plight of our people, we must look no further than the Scriptures where we will find some mind-blowing insight.

It is not just the black man who is under attack, it is the entire race. The Bible states that the man is the head of his household. If the house is to be destroyed, the head of the house becomes target, the first line of attack. Therefore, if the race is to be destroyed, the leaders must first be taken, leaving the house or the race vulnerable and helpless. In the Gospel of Mark 3:27, Jesus said the following: *"No man can enter into the house of a strong man and spoil his goods except he first bind the strong man, then he will spoil his goods."*

The very same sentiments are echoed in the Gospel of Matthew 12:29. If we place this in perspective concerning the black man and his goods, the question then becomes, what are the referred goods? What is a man's priced possession? One of the very first things God gave to man was his domain, the Garden of Eden (a place to stay) and then his wife, with a command to bring forth children, (family). If the enemy is to destroy the family, he must come after the head of the household; if he is to destroy a race, he goes after the leaders of the race. The men are the leaders of the race and thus are under attack, systematic or not, you can draw your own inferences on the subject.

Another dilemma also plaguing our society is the erosion of manly principles among men today. This may be attributed to the way manhood is defined today. I have often heard and concur with the saying that love is an action word; you do not simply speak love or speak of love but you do love. You express love, and you can feel it. Therefore, in the light of this, the question is this: *Is manhood something that is simply attained by reaching a certain number (age), or is it a qualification attained based on true and pure character, principle and responsibility?* Becoming a man is not on autopilot.

The Transition

As I ponder on what it really means to be a man, I am reminded of the words of the Apostle Paul as stated in 1Corinthians 13:11, *"When I was a child, I spoke as a child, I understood as a child, I thought as a child: but when I became a man, I put away childish things."* Apostle Paul acknowledges that there was a time when he had to break through the boundaries or the imaginary line that separate those two stages of life, that imaginary line that separates boys from men; but the question, therefore, is where do we draw that line? When does a boy become a man, and what prepares him for that transition?

That answer may vary based on culture and or tradition, but nonetheless, they all tend to speak of age. They speak solely of the numbers by which one is theoretically or legally identified as an adult or a man if you are a male; the only real difference being the age depending on the culture or statutes of the land. I would dare say, however, that although a male is legally identified as a man based on having attained a certain age, age is secondary to good character and good morals when it comes to manhood. So that being said, age is really not what qualifies a male as a man, but what really separates men from boys are the innate qualities of godly principles and character, developed by good upbringing and training. A boy may grow up to be an adult and still lack the true character of a real man.

As a boy transitions from juvenile to manhood, he must be cognizant of the fact that his life is about to change. He must realize that changes must be made and must be willing to make them. He must also understand that there will be challenges ahead; therefore, he must make a conscious decision to be not just numerically ready or physically ready, but he must also be spiritually ready, emotionally ready, and like the Apostle Paul says, he must be ready to put away all childish things.

As a good soldier prepares for battle, he girds himself in preparation to fight and ultimately win the battle. In the very same manner is a young man to prepare for the task as he embarks on the road to manhood. He must gird himself; embrace the challenges as they present themselves, overcoming one at a time for no one promised that the road was going to be easy.

Many of our young men today are growing up without fathers or good role models in their lives. Having a good role model provides for a strong foundation for a young man to build on as he makes the transition from boy to man. Studies show that there could be lasting psychological effects on children growing up without fathers and these psychological effects can have an outsized impact on whom they become later in life. Some of the effects of growing up without a father include:

- *Aggressive behavior towards others*
- *Low self-esteem*
- *Poor academic performance in school*
- *Depression*
- *Drug use*

In light of this fact, how is a boy to be taught or trained and prepared for manhood? In the face of this high rate of fatherless homes today, who is to teach the young males how to become real men? Can a mother do that? Very interesting question; therefore, let us explore.

Some may agree, some may disagree, and others may agree to disagree; I disagree to agree. To explain myself, let me allude to my earlier comments regarding what makes a boy a man. While I am in total agreement that a male child needs a male role model to teach and train him in manly things, we must, however, be prepared always and have a contingency plan in place. *"The boat does not sink just because the captain bailed out,"* but the second in command must take charge and steer to safety.

The second in command of the household is the mother and as I stated earlier, age is second place to true and pure character; therefore, character being the main ingredients can be instilled by any good mother in the absence of the father, no matter how difficult the struggle. Age comes naturally but character is developed by good upbringing. If a mother can develop good character in a son, then I think she can certainly prepare a boy for manhood. I am somewhat apprehensive, though, about what a mother can teach her son with respect to the physical realities of becoming a man, nonetheless, I believe that once good character has been set in place, the other physical attributes will follow naturally.

A Good Role Model

On the subject of role models, I am reminded of a very heated discussion, which I was part of when I visited London sometime in 1992. Sitting at the dinner table with my sibling sisters and other family members, the subject of a role model for my then young sons became a topic of discussion. It was about that era when Michael Jordan and other sports athletes were highly looked upon as role models for all young boys and girls.

While it is true that my sons admired Michael and aspired to be like him, *(though they were all vertically challenged),* I insisted that I and no one else was a role model for my sons. Of course, I came under heavy verbal artillery from my younger sibling sisters and cousins who thought that a role model meant someone on television. It meant someone with recognized societal status, and that I had no name or status in society to be considered a role model, even to my own sons. How sad and how unfortunate that our society has adopted that falsehood over truth, the counterfeit over the reality or the imaginary TV father over the real fathers at home! The ignorance, the misinformation and the lack of knowledge has contributed to this dilemma. It is therefore, incumbent on every one of us to take our rightful place in our homes to teach, train and mentor our young ones, equipping them with the required knowledge or the next generation will lose ground to the follies of the ignorant.

During that discussion, what I experienced was utter ignorance at best. I had no other option but to stand and fight against that misinformation with the hope that wisdom would eventually prevail, and the knowledge that if anyone was going to be a role model for my sons that was going to be me.

Having shared that experience with you, I think this would be a time quite fitting to share with you my thoughts on what I would deem to be a good role model. A good role model is selfless, one who is not only present but leads by example, he gives instructions; he sets a solid foundation and mentors others in a way that brightens the path to their future. If in your thoughts this sounds like I am describing a leader, you are not wrong at all because in essence, that is what a role model is. Therefore, the first role models that any child should know are his/her parents and obviously the father if the child is a male, in which case, the father must be present and available.

A role model is not an athlete, not an R&B artist, not a hip-hop or movie star as some would have you believe. In fact, it was NBA Hall of Famer Charles Barkley who came under criticism some time in 1993 when he made the following statement, *"I am not a role model; I am not paid to be a role model."* He continued, *"Parents should be role models. Just because I dunk a basketball doesn't mean I should raise your kids."*

What a strong statement to make, and what profound truth lies there in! I am in total agreement with this sentiment and strongly believe that no one is in a better position than you to raise or mentor your kids. These men have their lives to live and believe me, your kids are not their priority. They are paid professionals, some of which do not possess the needed character to be real men. You may make them your idols if you wish, but they are not your role models.

This was exactly the point I was attempting to make during that heated discussion with my siblings in England the year before. Who knew that a Hall of Famer in the person of Sir Charles Barkley would have come to endorse my position a year later?

<u>My Father is Absent</u>

Having established that the primary role model for a young man should be his father, I am sure that this gives rise to the argument regarding the presence or absence of the father in the home or for that matter, in the boy's life. There is no question that children need their fathers and boys in particular, have an even greater need for their father's presence and guidance. Nevertheless, I believe that there are always viable substitutes when the first line has become unavailable. Again, *the boat does not sink because the captain bails out.*

I'd like to appeal to the single mothers desiring to have a male role model in their son's lives and make the following recommendations. Your kids want to emulate a real man. They aspire to be great; somewhere deep inside of them, is a burning desire to be somebody, and though they may not be able to verbally express it, they have concerns about tomorrow, concerns about becoming a man, so here are some qualities to look for in a role model.

1). **Selflessness** – Choose a man who demonstrates the willingness to place the needs of others before his own; a man who understands that his part in a young man's life is as valuable as his own needs and would be willing to do whatever it takes to build him up.

2). **Love for others** – It won't be a fallacy on my part to suggest that selfishness and self-lovingness among men is the thing of the day. Men tend to be selfish and only love themselves. So in your quest for a role model for your son, be careful to choose one who clearly displays evidence of true love for humanity to the extent that he is willing to make sacrifices on their behalf. In the book of

Philippians 2:3, the Apostle Paul stated as follows, *"Do nothing out of selfish ambition or vain conceit but rather in humility, valuing others above yourself."*

3). **Love for God** – Choose a man who has learned to love God; a man who has shown that he is humble enough to operate under a greater authority that empowers him to face the daily challenges of life. A man who understands what it means to submit to a greater authority is a great example for young men to emulate. The fact is that if one is not under authority, he cannot be effective in authority. You cannot be a role model if you are not submissive. If you are not serving others selflessly, if you're not making sacrifices, then you're not fully walking in the true precepts of the intended plan for manhood.

Becoming a man is indeed a very difficult task and many juveniles enter that stage of life with a very nonchalant attitude, not really knowing what to expect or how to conduct themselves as men when they get there. Becoming a man is a tremendous responsibility that was involuntarily imposed on every male child, but if he is to be successful at it, he must possess good character, embrace good teachings and emulate a good role model.

As we speak of becoming a man, I would be remised if I did not mention that some of the outstanding characteristics of a man are his physical strength, size and masculinity. Men come in all sizes, heights and shapes. They were made to be physically strong and their size and strength can sometimes be misunderstood, even by those who possess them. If true character has not taken root in a juvenile who has grown to be of a large stature, he may tend to use those characteristic as a means of intimidation of others who are of a lesser stature. Hence, the reason a man should not be defined by his age, size, physical strength and masculinity but by the character, the softness and the love that he displays regardless of his physical stature. He may simply be a male adult.

Lost amid all the chaos and the rubble of society is the role of a man. Over the years, lots have changed whereas gender roles have switched; men are staying home caring for the children while the mothers go out there and grind the mills to bring home the bacon. In some cases, they have been made to forcefully vacate their prized possessions, belittled, ridiculed and de-masculinized, sometimes even by their significant others who fail to allow them to function in their roles, causing them to lose themselves and their sense of purpose.

Having been a police officer for a while, I have seen my share of dysfunctional and broken families. I have seen fathers so powerless in the homes, unable to correct a juvenile son without mom's interruption. I have seen the male ego virtually broken, crushed and nearly destroyed. Often we talk of domestic violence and seldom see that from the perspective of the male victim. If we are not careful and watchful, the enemy will use our very own against us. The plan is to destroy at any cost. When Satan came into the garden as stated in the book of Genesis, he did not approach Adam but used his significant other against him. This strategy of Satan has not changed. He will attempt to use the weaker vessel or whomever he can in his efforts to destroy the family. I have seen some broken men. I have seen some "gentle" men, too humble and too respectful to even speak up sometimes. These men are ultimately chased out of their domain and forced to relinquish their roles in the home leaving vulnerable juveniles behind to face uncertain futures.

How can a juvenile know what his role is when he becomes a man if Daddy has not been there to demonstrate that? How can he envision a bright future with such a cloud of uncertainty hovering over his mind, created by the absence of the one whose responsibility it is to guide him? Let's face it my brothers! The way he looks at the world and sees the future is undoubtedly affected by his observation of the above stated issues. Men must not only return to their roles in their homes and in society, but they must be allowed to carry them out. No man is perfect but we can all strive towards that goal with effort, determination and character. It has been said that when we do our best, not even angels can do better.

My appeal, therefore, is to all that are concerned about the future of our young men, to those who would like to see better family structures and better communities with stronger leadership. I strongly urge that we all take every necessary step to place things in perspective. Let's work harder on "Plan A," keeping the fathers in the home; and if by reason of some unfortunate circumstances he happens to be absent, the ship must continue to sail with super mom in the captain's seat. Finally, yet importantly, Mom, be careful to make good choices when choosing a role model for your children.

~Dedication~

I would like to dedicate a portion of this chapter to the following young men, whom I have had the pleasure of raising and mentoring over the years. Some of them have seamlessly made the transition from boyhood to manhood and it is my hope and prayer that they all cross that imaginary line some day and become productive men contributing to the betterment of our society.

Dean Durand

Shirlon Durand

Wayne Durand

Savion Ali "Little Vern" Durand

I'm sure you have probably guessed the family relation by now, but in case you missed it, the first three are my sons and then my first grandson.

My Adopted Sons:

Kevon Ross, Antoine Bent, Timothy Duhaney, Johnny Duhaney, Kymani Leon and Kyshawn Williams

I am very proud of all of you. It is my prayer that the grace of God never ceases to cover you all for the rest of your lives.

Biography of Walt Harris

Walt Harris, a retired NFL Pro Bowler, spent an impressive 13 years in the NFL. Walt was selected by the Chicago Bears as the 13th overall draft pick in the 1st Round of the 1996 NFL Draft. Over his 13 NFL seasons, Harris played for four different franchises, including the Chicago Bears, Indianapolis Colts, Washington Redskins, and San Francisco 49ers. He finished his professional career with 2007 NFC Defensive player of the week and month and earned a 2007 Pro Bowl Player nominee.

Harris is a 2012 SEC Legends Inductee, 2017 Mississippi State Hall of Fame Inductee, 2018 Ring of Honor Inductee at Mississippi State and the interception record-holder. Harris transferred his football prowess on the field into the overarching themes of spirituality, family life, friendships, and community service. He is the founder of Official Pro Players Inc. a 501C3 nonprofit organization, a global network of professional athletes from all sports, who come together to remain socially active, socially responsible, and involved in its communities.

With the mission to engage, unite, and empower the sports community, Harris founded Official Pro Players Inc. (OPP) to help build, support, and connect athletes in their local communities. Its mission is to raise funds through awareness for various causes worldwide. OPP is the only organization that unites current and retired athletes from all sports, both male and female. Harris is also an advocate for domestic violence. He has great compassion for the victims and survivors and takes an unapologetic stand against this wrongful act. Harris serves as Vice President of the Former Players Atlanta Chapter. His passion for men to connect and build each other up in faith, accountability and support inspired him to conduct a weekly Morning Prayer line called "Kings to Kings Prayer Call."

He is a motivational speaker with a passion in the real-estate sector and finding various investment opportunities to increase his wealth. In addition to being an accomplished athlete, a visionary, and philanthropist, Harris is a proud father of five.

Personal Profile

Key Words
Engage, Unite, Empower, Love

Favorite Quote
As a man think in his heart so is he. (Proverbs 23:7)

Values
Relationship, Honesty, Youth, Community

Marketable Skills
Public Speaking, Networking

Contact Information
Email: info@officialproplayers.com

Website: www.officialproplayers.org

LinkedIn.com: Walt Harris

Facebook: facebook.com/waltharris

MY PEOPLE PERISH
FOR LACK OF KNOWLEDGE

Walt Harris

As a professional athlete for over 13 years, I had the benefit to see many places and meet many interesting people. However, one of the most eye-opening experiences was the realizations that being a male was just a start to developing into a man. Therefore, one of the critical factors to catapult me into my journey into becoming a man was to learn how important it was to live a well-rounded lifestyle. Growing up as the youngest of 13 siblings, my parents had only a 5th grade education, and a home that was just big enough to accommodate a family of four. Discussions were scarce to none on the topic of health. A healthy lifestyle in my house meant having enough food on the table to feed everyone. Healthy was also measured by whether one went in to visit the doctor or not. Unfortunately, this type of childhood thinking hurdled its way all throughout my adolescent and high school years. Even many of the same beliefs at the time while playing sports at the collegiate level had its own limits and similar limitations. While living up to the expectations of being a male,

64

exhibiting the features and the title, I was still on my journey of embracing the process of becoming a man. I had to understand that manhood was not as instantaneous as it seemed and it was not as simple. Similar to a cook who has found the right ingredients to create his dish, he must wait as the heat turns what is unfinished into a final masterpiece. Manhood is the development from a little boy to a man whereby his ability to ascertain to the temperature of circumstances and trials develop him into a mature and whole man.

At a very young age, I was known in my household of many siblings as the one who smiled a lot, didn't say much at school, and could run fast. I was sometimes the teacher's favorite in class while winning first place ribbons and trophies at field day for my class. This continued from pre-K all the way up to elementary. I knew my dad as a hard worker who was skilled at driving tractors that built highways, which went all the way into the city of Atlanta. My dad was the main discipliner in the home. Therefore, we knew where he stood and what the rules were. My mom didn't have a particular skill; however she worked whatever job necessary to help pay the bills. Working two jobs with long hours, I sometimes waited up late for her to arrive home. My dad and mom separated during my high school years but never divorced. Looking back as a teenager is quite interesting as we think we know what is best for us, but we had much to learn. When my dad left home, we personally saw his departure as an opportunity to have more freedom not knowing how serious the impact would have on our personal lives. Hence, the rules went out the door and so did we.

What was absolutely forbidden became easily permissible as we began to bend the rules by staying out much later than the norm. Look backing, this time was a pivotal moment in my life that could have cost me opportunities for future successes. I realized that the absence of authority could have birthed the lack of accountability and discipline needed in my life during that time.

Thankfully, sports became my filler and path that helped me to give birth to what I was on the verge of aborting. Although the house rules continued to be ignored, I couldn't ignore the rules while on the field which demanded accountability and discipline and that became my foundation of manhood. With so many distractions in the world today, it is vital for teenagers to have the right guidance and structure in their lives. These things can help guard against the empty white noise that can so easily hinder and delay a young man's journey into becoming a man. After a while, with enough success on the field, God created an opportunity for me to earn a college scholarship to attend Mississippi State University.

My college experience was much of the same structure and order; however, the change of environment was new to me. Although being away from home took some adjusting, it undoubtedly prepared me to embrace change later on in my professional career. An essential part of the process of becoming a man is learning how to adapt to change.

After being drafted by the Chicago Bears in 1996, my journey to becoming a more whole healthy individual began its course as my access to new people and new ways of thinking evolved. This was another critical factor of me embracing manhood. Although playing at the highest level professionally and having a platform that many people admired, the prestige of the NFL did not replace the knowledge I needed to make me whole.

Playing defensive cornerback in the NFL required a specific discipline and focused necessary to keep up with the elusive offensive players and crafty coordinators every weekend. Our job was to defend at whatever cost to stay on the field in such a competitive position. The better I performed as an athlete, the longer we continued to play. However, my knowledge on the field did not replace the need of wisdom off the field concerning wholeness. I was defending what could win a game, but my lack of complete self-care ultimately could cause me to lose in life. I had to put in the work if I wanted to live a more full life. I began to realize that my mental, physical, and spiritual well-being was what I needed for an ultimate win. The Apostle Paul explains this process quite simple in biblical terms in 1 Corinthians 13:11. *"When I was a child I spoke, I thought, and I reasoned like a child, but when I became a man, I put childish things away."* This ladies and gentlemen, in my opinion, demonstrates the correct process of manhood. It starts with the way one thinks. How a man thinks is an indication of what stage of manhood he is in.

Therefore, as we continue to mature as men, we must begin to change the way we think. When I graduated from high school and began to experience life as a student at Mississippi State University, I brought with me some of the same prepossessions I carried from high school. It didn't take long until the new climate of the college lifestyle demanded a new outlook and a higher expectation of me to clothe myself with the necessary growth to succeed. If we are to grow as men, we must first be willing to change our environment that commands a new advanced way of thinking. However, it is also important to note that a new environment is not all that is required of us to grow. We also must be willing to humble ourselves and be ready to adapt to that environment so we can mature and evolve. All throughout my high-school, college, and professional career I've seen many individuals drop the ball by failing to accept change. Change is sometimes hard but necessary for growth, and we must be willing to embrace it; knowing what God is trying to build in us. Playing football on the professional level came with many changes on the field and off. When we think about 1 Corinthians 13:11, Paul decides to do away with the old way of doing things referencing it as childlike thinking.

Transitioning from team to team, family lifestyle modifications, and continuing to allow God to mold me into a better man caused me to have a productive way of thinking and a new way of doing things. Changing teams randomly and sometimes unexpectedly became the norm for a professional athlete. If one is not mentally aware and prepared to handle the change, it could lead to many struggles and challenges of adapting. As a man embraces change with a positive mindset, I believe it puts him in a better place to see and maximize the opportunity that God has before him. I had to do away with my old thought patterns, my comfort zone, and what was widely accepted to transition into the man I wanted to be. Ultimately, if we are going to embrace manhood, we have to take God's way of doing things. God says, "My people perish for lack of knowledge" (Hosea 4:6). Obtaining new information contrary or beyond what we understand is vital to surviving the gravitational pull to keep us the same. As men, we are jerked in many directions, and the world is continuously changing and telling us what manhood really is. However, I came to realize the path to manhood would always end when we know where we ultimately started.

My start began when I met a new teammate in Chicago. His consistent lifestyle of peace and order created enough curiosity in me to want to know more. Over time and continuously gaining information, I finally gave my life to God. This began my understanding and knowledge of a new level of manhood. I realized that in being a male, I only needed to exist; however, being a man I needed to apply biblical principles. Those principles put me on the right path as I continued to grow. I made it a habit to submerge myself under biblical teachings and around people that were hungry and consistent as I was to improve my inner man. Not really realizing the full effect of the consistency I created within, I was on my journey to becoming a better me. However, on my trip to becoming a more well-rounded man, it did not keep me from many obstacles and shortcomings. After many years of what seemed to appear progression, my life took a significant fall. After being married for many years, I went through an unfortunate divorce. The family life I knew was gone, and the responsibility of being an impactor in the home was no more. The physical disconnection from my kids also played a toll on me as a man. The separation and loss were extremely stressful as I began to lose my grip slowly. The idea of letting others down took me into a private place of condemnation and guilt as it resulted in a lot of hurt and pain for everyone. Darkness was all around which attracted more darkness. Bad decisions bred more of the same. Lost in a place, far from where I once was, all I knew was to remember never to stop believing. All the years of meditation on what I understood from God's Word had its tests. But there were specific promises that I knew I would never let go and that was knowing that God was always with me. Nevertheless, the voices in my head kept reminding me of the choices I had made which caused me not to receive God's grace. I was forgiven, but I had not forgiven myself. Many people deal subconsciously with the inability to forgive themselves. Therefore, it causes a place of stagnation. This is similar to a pond that doesn't have an entry or exit point to release impure toxins. Thus you get an extreme build-up of non-fresh water.

God desires to be that exit point for us where we can let go and find rest in Him. 1 Peter 5:7 says, *"Cast all your worries and cares on him for he cares for you."* I had to learn through the encumbrances of life that we will face many setbacks, but it's during those lapses we find our greatest comebacks as we continue to seek higher knowledge and standards in God. There are many distractions that man will face and encounter to keep one from coming into the understanding of the truth. I have found that if I focus on the bigger picture, my ending will always be bright. Over the years, my game plan for life is *Canceling Out Distractions Early and Keep It Moving* (CODEKIM). Please feel free to use #CODEKIM anytime a distraction comes your way. Distractions are anything or anyone that comes to deter you from becoming into the full knowledge of all who God wants you to be. When we come into the understanding of who God created us to be, we will become confident, whole and purposeful.

As we look around and view many sectors today, many people are perishing, but not for lack of money, possessions, or opportunity, but because of a lack of knowledge. Things no one can take from you is faith, experiences, and understanding. Allow these things to inspire you on your journey to manhood.

~Dedication~

Brandon Harris

Jason Towns

Jaden Perry

Charles McCormick

Leo Dorsey

Jason Huzzie

Elijah Towns

Landon Towns

Andre Towns

Tom Carter

Biography of Dalton Kornegay, PhD

Dalton Kornegay, PhD, IMFTT, CPBC, CCCH is also the Founder and President of Faith Connected Mentoring Ministries (FCMM). In his capacity with FCMM, he is an integrated marriage and family temperament counselor. His driven mission is to help make a difference in marriages and families that are plagued by despairing issues that rip away at the fabric of God ordained family lives. Under the banner of FCMM are two additional faith-based non-profit 501(C) (3) entities – Men of Change Inc. (adult males) and Mentoring For Change Inc. (youth).

He has a post-secondary education (Doctorate/ Master) with certification/ licensure in Temperament Counseling. Also holds an undergraduate degree in Biology and Chemistry with special interest in Industrial Pharmaceutical Innovation & Technology.

As a civilian, he is a Principal GMP Compliance Consultant as the President of Mentoring For Change Consulting Agency, Inc. Dr. Kornegay is married to Genea Kornegay for 24 years and has one daughter. In addition, he is a Certified Personality & Behavioral Consultant, Therapeutic Mentoring Coach for Boys of Standard and Success, a Professional Christian Life Coach and Mentor Trainer with over 21 years of experience in leading others to transformation. He is a Certified Christian Chaplain, and a licensed and ordained Elder in the ministry of Jesus Christ. He is a veteran of the US Army/ Active Reserve with over 23 years of operation, administration and training experience.

Personal Profile

Key Words

Impacting and helping people to change their life in order to save their life!

Favorite Quote

"What does love look like? It has the hands to help others. It has the feet to hasten to the poor and needy. It has eyes to see misery and want. It has ears to hear the sighs and sorrows of men. That is what love looks like." ~ Saint Augustine

Values

- Address issues that affect personal and spiritual development
- Development of responsibility to lead self, family and others
- Maximize opportunities given for advancement
- Make a positive impact in the world in which you live
- Know the will of God & Be determined to carry it out!

Marketable Skills

Temperament Counselor, Certified Personality & Behavioral Consultant, Professional Christian Life Coach and Mentor Trainer, Licensed and ordained Elder in the Ministry of Jesus Christ and Certified Christian Chaplain

Contact Information

Email: daltonkornegay.phd@gmail.com
Website: www.menofchange.us
LinkedIn.com: Dalton Kornegay, PhD
Facebook/ Twitter: menofchangeinc

74

UNDERSTANDING THE IMPORTANCE AND INTRICACIES OF MANHOOD

Dalton Kornegay, PhD

I grew up in a two-parent home in the rural south of North Carolina. At a very early age, I was inspired to be honest, work hard, take responsibility for my actions and be accountable in my community. I grew in a family of seven brothers and sisters. My father was a stern disciplinarian and my mother ran a very tight ship within our home. These kinds of conditions left very little room for slothfulness and error. By default, I was influenced to be a winner and treat others with dignity and respect that I wanted and required. Therefore, it can be noted that even today I am still someone who is respectful, responsible, accountable and inspired to continue to excel. In my past, I made many mistakes along the way. In fact, some were very costly! However, I would take nothing for my journey of mistakes and shortcomings for it helped make me to be who I am today. I have an inner uncanny knack to succeed in whatever I do in life. In my circle of influence as a seasoned man of God, not only do I share what I have read and come to understand but also

75

what I know through personal experiences. Now let's segue into the topic at hand, which is to take a deeper look at what real manhood in the 21st century is all about.

Let's start by looking at some glaring statistics:

- Children that grow up without an involved father venture on to be engrossed by poverty, become high school dropouts, experience teen pregnancy and teen fatherhood, use illicit drugs, experience unhealthy emotional, health, and behavioral issues, suffer abuse, and engage in various forms of criminal activity.

- Men who do no respect their wives or significant others in most cases – son(s) will have a proclivity to disrespect women.

- In 2005, over 11.2% of men in America used illicit substances; 7.4% were fathers.

- In 2007, 1 out of 12 fathers in America with children from ages 12 to 17, suffered from alcohol or drug depended disorders.

- Seventy-eight percent of poor unmarried fathers believe it is okay to cohabitate.

- Only 18.8% of residential fathers in America are involved with their children's daily activities.
- Ninety-three percent of men in prison have fathered at least one child, finding it extremely difficult to re-integrate into society due to the inability to find a job with a decent wage, without completing some form of re-directional/support program.

According to the aforementioned statistics, it is apparent that manhood in America is in crisis and is not working the way that God originally intended. There are multiple reasons for this deficit but I believe it gives more justice to focus on what it is needed and how to go about it versus focusing on the negative.

The gravity of this situation is of such that men must be given the environment and a platform to address their personal issues and/or spiritual underdevelopment. Men also have to be empowered with the sense of responsibility to lead their families and make a positive impact on the community. It is widely understood that very few men are afforded the direct exposure to proper manhood leadership training. This universal issue must first be acknowledged in order to adequately address it, in order to help men become "true priests of their homes and reign in their environments as kings."

Men have to be taught how to prioritize, focus on life challenges and search out re-directional strategies that help them to get back on track when a crisis or misfortune takes place. The issue is that it is hard to emulate something that you have no exposure to. For example, a holistic approach should take place when something happens to enable an individual to acknowledge the issue(s) he may be experiencing primarily and then move to determine the root cause. Men today have to be ushered to place in their respective lives to see the need for leadership, mentoring, and coaching to help positively change where they are to help them get to ultimately where they need to be. Everyone in life needs someone to be accountable to and have someone to confide in. God did not make man to live on an island to himself. However, mankind was made to be a communal people that lived together with respect to symbiotic relationships. Meaning men should always help each other as he is empowered to do so.

It is very important that society gets it right and help men to be restored to their rightful place as true leaders. There is work that must be done by all. We have to respect each other as a human race regardless of color, background or upbringing. There is a level of respect that has gotten lost in society where many feel it is okay to say whatever or do whatever. I beg the difference, and the reason why is because when you say things and/or do things that affects others that is a problem. We have to get back to the basics of treating others the way we want to be treated. Each one has to reach one. Every man should feel compelled to pour into and help make a difference in someone else's life. This confirms the true essence of "Paying It Forward." When you see something, say something. We as men and as a people have gotten too lax in the mindset of "if it does affect me, it is not my business." However, where would be today as a society if that was the mindset of our forefathers? We cannot afford to rest on that kind of thinking any longer. If injustice, murder, rape, questionable acts or other actions that are un-becoming occur in your midst, you must stand and speak truth to power. In closing, this is the true of essence of manhood for the 21st century.

~Dedication~

Solomon Jones, Maysville, NC

Marvin Witherspoon, San Diego, CA

James Franks, Rock Hill, SC

Arthur Kornegay Jr, Wallace, NC

Nathaniel Rogers, Greenville, NC

Terrence Elliott Sr, Elizabethtown, KY

Lynwood Kornegay, Kinston, NC (Posthumous)

Arthur Kornegay Sr, Dover, NC (Posthumous)

Biography of Jason Jerome McFarlane

 **Jason Jerome McFarlane**, husband, father, youth leader, and managing director. Born in the U.S. capital, Washington, D.C., Jason made his debut on May 8, 1986.

Growing up in the Montgomery County Maryland, Jason had his hopes set on becoming a businessman. During his course of high school, Jason became interested in civil engineering. He shared that he always dreamed of developing a city in which he and his friends could live and own their own businesses. After seeking a Civil Engineering degree at Morgan State University, Jason moved from Maryland to join his mother in Kissimmee, Florida. It was there that he was introduced to real estate and began a career of a real estate agent. After spending some time in the real estate arena, Jason felt like the timing was off, and joined Top Star Autos. He thrived there and became one of the key players to their business.

During the course of time as a car salesman, he met his wife, LaToya. The two developed a friendship in which they became inseparable. The pair later married and Jason became the father of two girls. As a dedicated father, Jason often attends school volunteer programs consistently promoting hands-on activities with his children. He always had a love for the community and a desire to do more for youth.

Jason and his family later joined Divine Visitation International Ministries and became active in the church. With God's favor and encouragement from leadership, he was given the opportunity to become a Minister of Music and is now playing the bass guitar. Jason and his wife went on to serve as youth leaders; mentoring teens to help strive to have a better perspective on life.

During the transition of moving from Florida to Georgia, Jason began to try to find other ways to provide for his family. He had several career titles; from real estate agent to car salesman, he had made his way to become an insurance agent. He sought out different companies in which he learned a lot yet he wanted to do more. Jason soon planted his feet at Genesis Asset Management Strategies Group and became the managing director for the company. He now provides financial assistance to doctors, lawyers, pastors, celebrities, business owners, and the list goes on.

Personal Profile

Key Words

Persevere - continue in a course of action even in the face of difficulty or with little or no prospect of success.

Grit - courage and resolve; strength of character.

Effort - a vigorous or determined attempt.

Favorite Quote

"He that is good for making excuses is seldom good for anything else." ~ Benjamin Franklin

Values

Integrity, Perseverance, Loyalty, and Family

Marketable Skills

Problem Solving, Adaptability, Interpersonal, Teamwork, Leading

Contact Information

Email: mcfarlanejason@gmail.com
LinkedIn: Jason McFarlane
Instagram: @moneymattersphp

LOST IN GREATNESS

Jason McFarlane

I'll never forget the sound of my mother's cries as she pulled up to see me her only son, the one she worked so hard to raise, handcuffed in the back of a police car. I knew I was wrong and took responsibility for that. But seeing my mother in agony crying as I sat there not able to do anything but watch, hurt me far more than my situation.

"Let me out please," I told the officer.

"I can't do that," he replied.

"Look you already have me in handcuffs and look at how many of you there are out here. I'm not running anywhere. Please just let me out for a few seconds."

"I'm sorry, but I can't do that," he restated.

"You see the lady that just pulled up?" I asked. "That's my mother. If you don't let me out and give me a few seconds to talk to her and calm her down, you're going to have to call an ambulance to take her to the hospital. It's already bad enough. Please just let me out so I can calm her down," I pleaded.

He looked hard at me in the rear view mirror and I guess felt I was sincere and let me out. Yeah, I was able to calm her down some, but as I sat back in my former position in the police car, all I could think was, "how could this happen to me?! People get locked up every day, but *me*? This isn't for me. I should never have been here." Getting to the facility and having my fingerprints taken, then seeing myself in an orange jumpsuit made it even worse. The disgrace, the shame, rock bottom… How *did* I get here?

Like many, I grew up in the church. Every service, every practice, every event, every outing, I was there. I was probably at church or at a church event more hours a week than some spend at a part-time job. Children's choir, I sang. Teen Talent, I was there. Church camp, every year (I was baptized every year there too). Church basketball team, I was on it. Church soundboard, I helped run it. Revivals, couldn't miss those. General Assembly, I was at those as well. District church meetings, there. Drama team, oh yeah I acted too. The problem was I acted too well. One foot in and one foot out. I'm grateful that one foot was in though. If it wasn't, I wouldn't be here today. Although I was young, I knew how to move in my surroundings. My mother made sure of that. I was not going to be embarrassing her or making a fool of myself in public. She had this look that would stop me in my tracks. She'd be in the choir and look down to see me doing something questionable. There was "the look". I'd be out in public and start doing something crazy and boom, the look. No matter where we went or how far away she was in the room, one look, and like magic, I would stop immediately. The thing is, my mother would work up to three jobs at a time and wasn't always able to give me that look.

When I got some time alone or was able to spend time with my friends, I was a completely different kid. I used to have a bad temper and loved to fight. There were a few times I fought at church. I fought at school during recess numerous times per week. I'd fight with my cousin or one of my older "brothers" just to learn more techniques and get tougher. I was the youngest of them all so figured if I could hold my ground against them, I'd be in good shape around anyone my age. I had an issue with identifying manhood. Without a male figure in the household, often times I looked toward what society projected a black male to be. I had to be tough. I had to be involved in crime. I had to have a lot of women around me. I had to get fast money. I had to be good at sports. These were mandatory from what I had seen on television and in the movies. So, I started lining myself up to meet the criteria. The church boy that was prophesied to become a preacher ran far away from that as Jonah did with Nineveh before getting eaten by the great fish.

Instead of following the older brothers and the father figures their dads were to me, I decided I'd make my own path. My sister moved out of the state a little before I graduated from high school and my mother did as well. Growing up, we were all we had. Now, with them gone, it was time to be a man. I stopped going to church and removed myself from a lot of the church figures I had grown up around. I found myself, judging my manhood based off of the criteria society had shown me. I got an apartment with the girl I was dating at the time and still found myself chasing after other women. In order to provide for one's home, you have to have money. Although I was working, you could *never* have too much money, so I did things to make extra money on the side. Men drink, smoke, and have plenty of women. I had to check those boxes off too. Although I was paying to go to school, I had stopped going. As smart as I was, as much talent as I had, as great of a support system I grew up around, I let it all slip away and got distracted by what I thought manhood was supposed to be. I was driving down a path of self-destruction and flooring the gas the whole way.

If you couldn't tell from all of the church activity I spoke about earlier, my mother is a God-fearing woman. One of the things she was blessed with was the ability to hear from God through dreams. I would get call after call after call from her asking if everything was okay and telling me about how she didn't like the dreams she was having. Once she told me about a dream she had that was an exact reflection of what I had going on in my life at the time. Yet, I was busy being a man and she would never understand that. I just told her the dream sounded crazy and nothing like that was going on. About a month later, I got the phone call.

"Hey Ma! How's everything going?" I asked

"Everything is okay," she responded. "I just wanted to let you know that it's time for you to move down here with me. I've been having these dreams and just do not like what I am seeing. It's time for you to pack up all your stuff and put it in the car. You can drive the car to the train station, put the car on the train, and ride the train down."

"I'm not doing that Ma," I replied. "I have my place here. I like being here. There is nothing for me there. I'm just not interested. In addition to that, I still have about a month before the semester is done."

"I bought your ticket," she replied. "You are packing the stuff up in the car. I arranged for people to help you. You are leaving your apartment and staying with a friend of the family. You will stay there until you get on the train and travel down here."

I got off the phone dumbfounded. I had no intention of moving anywhere but couldn't tell her that. I was not going to start an argument with my mother for any reason. She would just have to see that we agree to disagree on that one. I went on about my business, but my mind couldn't get off of the conversation. I started reflecting and realized I wasn't going to school. I wasn't living right. I put myself at risk many, many times. What was really working in my favor? As I was contemplating everything, I received another phone call.

"What's up boy?" the familiar voice asked.

"Not much fam! What's going on with you?" was my reply.

"Get all your stuff packed," he said. "We're going to be out there tomorrow to help you move everything out and you're going to be staying with me until you head down with your mother."

All I could say was, "Okay," but still, in my head, I was saying "Not happening!"

I took some time to reflect and began wondering what reason I had for staying? After thinking about it all, maybe a move was the best thing for me. It was time to start packing. It was time to rebuild the foundation. After moving back in with my mother, I had time to reflect and realized that a lot of the people that I had in my circle were not really in my corner. I began distancing myself from everyone and analyzing why everyone around me was there. The people that I found to be true, I decided to stay in contact with. They say, "You can't move forward looking backwards." I began to realize that this was true. I was in a new surrounding and cut myself off from all of the negativity but still looked back at my past and wanted to recreate it. Look how God works though. I got myself involved in the same activities I was able to escape from. Only this time, I was smarter about it or at least I thought I was.

One day a girl questioned me on why I was doing what I was doing. My response was simple, "I don't see anything wrong with it and having more money never hurts." Her questioning sparked something in my brain though. That evening I remember driving back to the house and I said a prayer. During my time of talking to God, I let Him know that I honestly didn't see what was wrong with my actions. I asked Him to show me if what I was doing was wrong. A few days later, I learned that God answers prayers and the way He answers is not always what you had in mind. As I sat there in my orange jumpsuit, all I kept thinking was, "I guess there *was* something wrong with what I was doing." It was there, at my darkest point, that I started to change. It's funny how your worst moments can actually be the best moments of your life. I changed my ways and more importantly, changed my mindset. I met a girl and started going to church with her. The services were nothing like anything I had ever encountered and the pastor truly taught me some valuable lessons both biblically and in everyday life. I got married, and God started to move again.

I wasn't doing anything wrong, but everything in my life started shifting. Everything began falling apart for me. Things at my job started deteriorating and I got fired for the first time in my life. It put me in a continual cycle of dead-end jobs. I prayed and prayed and prayed but things got tougher financially and caused me to lose my home. I had to move my wife and kids into another person's home and we all slept on a mattress on the floor. It could have been much worse; at least we had a place to stay and try to regroup. However, it didn't happen.

Things just continued to get worse. I got pulled over and harassed by some cops. After a good 20 minutes of them pressing me about something I clearly wasn't involved in, they let me go. As they began to leave, they notified me that my license was suspended and if I got pulled over by another officer, there was a good chance of me going to jail. I hadn't gotten any tickets so it didn't make sense to me. "If my license was really suspended, why didn't they arrest me?" I thought to myself. I just viewed it as them trying to play more mind games to throw me off. I got home, checked my license online and sure enough, I was driving on a suspended license. About a year prior, I had cosigned on a car and the driver ran so many tolls without paying that my license was now suspended. At my dead end job, one of the girls who worked with me tried to get me fired and told management things that were far from the truth. Luckily, everything at that job was on camera or audibly recorded. After reviewing everything, they found no merit to what she said and I was able to keep the job. She made the job uncomfortable and with everything else falling out of whack in my life, I decided it was time to move. The place I had run to get away from the drama was no longer a drama-free place.

I took the little money I had, paid to get my license reinstated and got out of there. Even in my new surroundings, I found myself slipping farther away from God. I was going to church, yes, but it wasn't something I was growing from. In fact, for the most part, it made me revert back to some of my old ways and made me not want to be in church anymore. Sometimes I would get in moods where I just didn't want to be around anyone. Those were my "leave me alone and let me be" days. I was working from home at the time and my wife came in from work saying she needed me to go to the store with her. I didn't want to and flat out told her "no." She knew what she wanted, had the money to get it, had hands to be able to put them into the cart and transfer them into the car. Why was I needed? She insisted I go and to avoid an argument, I went. While at the store, I noticed an older lady who would not stop staring at me. I looked away and turned my back to her, but when I turned back, she was still there and still staring. When I had to walk past her, she stopped me.

I didn't want to talk to anyone, but just to be respectful, I stopped to entertain her. She began talking to me, telling me about how I looked like a nice young man of God and took the time to tell me about how beautiful my daughters were. I thanked her and tried to get away but she kept talking. I stayed and ended up getting invited to her church. She was trying to tell me where her church was located and I figured this would be my chance to have my wife take my place so I could go back to being alone. I let her know I had no idea where she was talking about and told her I would go get my wife so she could get the information. I left, found my wife, and brought her back to get the information. But as I tried to walk away, somehow the lady was able to give my wife the information and let her walk off, as I was still stuck there talking with this lady. It took my wife coming back to notify me that it was time to go and she had already paid for everything to get me away from this woman, but God knew what He was doing.

That following Sunday, we attended the church and things began to shift. A gentleman walked through the door and I had no idea who he was, but for whatever reason, I felt I needed to connect with him. As the service went on, I realized he was actually one of the pastors of the church. I listened to his sermon and some of the things he was saying directly correlated with my life. At the end of the service, everyone was standing up for the final prayer. I had blown my knee out a few years prior and it was bothering me so I decided to sit and pray. While praying, I felt someone come and tap me on the shoulder and say, "Come with me." Tired from the previous night and kind of lost in prayer, I didn't really comprehend or realize what was going on. I sat there continuing to pray and felt another tap and again heard the voice say, "Come with me." I opened my eyes and looked up to see the pastor I felt I needed to connect with and stood up. He led me to the front of the congregation and began speaking to me. He prophesied over my life and said some of the same things that were prophesied to me as a child. He spoke on some of the things that were directly going on in my life at that time and I was truly dumbfounded. I had just met this man and never had a conversation with him. How could he possibly know?

He prayed over me and as I was about to turn to walk away, he looked me in the eyes and said something that truly stuck. "You know what your problem is?" he asked. "You have a problem with belief. The moment you stop doubting everything and truly start believing, things will rapidly shift in your life." I analyzed his words and saw how true my problem with believing actually was. That day changed my life and his words began to shape my future. I kept attending church and began getting myself back on track with God. Being there also led me to an opportunity to meet another gentleman who I have connected with. It blessed me to be in the position to have my words read by you today. In addition, I have had a serious love for music my entire life and played instruments as a child. Now, I am a Minister of Music at the church and playing the bass guitar for the Lord. I have always had a big heart so much so that it has oftentimes gotten me into situations. One of the things I aspired to do was create a platform in which I can reach back and help other young men growing up today, in hopes to not experience some of the things I did. I am now a Youth Director at the church. I went from dead-end job to dead-end job to now being an executive of a soon to be multi-million-dollar insurance brokerage and financial firm. I have always used writing as an outlet and had the desire to write a book and now my words are being read today. God changes things. It's crazy what a little bit of faith and surrendering to your Maker can do.

Jeremiah 29: 11-14

11 For I know the plans I have for you," declares the Lord, "plans to prosper you and not to harm you, plans to give you hope and a future. 12 Then you will call on me and come and pray to me, and I will listen to you. 13 You will seek me and find me when you seek me with all your heart. 14 I will be found by you," declares the Lord, "and will bring you back from captivity. [b] I will gather you from all the nations and places where I have banished you," declares the Lord, "and will bring you back to the place from which I carried you into exile."

~Dedication~

Space was limited, but to all of the influential men in my life,
I thank you!

Stephen Gayle, New York, NY
Christian Sullivan, Gaithersburg, MD
David Early, Silver Spring, MD
Jerry Elder, Cleveland, TN
Jeff Robinson, Plant City, GA
Audley Gayle, Clarksburg, MD
Eli Ormsby, Gaithersburg, MD
Oniel Ormsby, Montgomery Village, MD
Matthieu Mars, Kissimmee, FL
Steven St. Hilaire, Kissimmee, FL
Marvin Jackson, Orlando, FL
Leroy Watts, Orlando, FL
Paul Severson, Davenport, FL
Michael Sanchez, Kissimmee, FL
Richard Welch, Cummings, GA
Noble Ibe, Grayson, GA
Ricardo Osbourne, Athens, GA
Calvin Ellison, Stone Mountain, GA
Nedrick Ambersley, Germantown, MD
Karl Richmond, Kissimmee, FL
Randy Baker, Arnold, MD
Kevin Webb, Stockbridge, GA
Gyasi Dennis, Gaithersburg, MD
Paul Ormsby, Frederick, MD
Chris Ashley, Frederick, MD

Biography of Keon Reid

Born in Jamaica, **Keon Reid** has grown into a vibrant and dynamic motivational teacher whose goal is to empower today's youth to become their best selves. Known for his jovial temperament and love for competition, Keon naturally gravitates to forming new relationships. He has earned his Master of Science in Computational Chemistry from Emory University and now works as a Capture Marketing Professional (Proposal Manager) at First Data, the world's largest merchant acquirer and payment processor.

Throughout his studies, Keon has published his research in scientific journals, spoken at local and national conferences and received many awards, with his most notable being the National Science Foundation GRFP Fellowship, one of the nation's most prestigious graduate honors. Keon has also served on numerous boards; he was voted on as the youngest sitting member of his church's Executive Board at the age of 23. With years of teaching and involvement in STEM, Keon is dynamically positioned to speak to students at different levels from K-12 and in higher education. He recently had the honor of speaking as the convocation speaker at the 2018 Honors College Convocation at Georgia State University, his alma mater.

Keon believes that this generation is uniquely positioned to influence their world at large through the right decisions. In order to champion change, one must demonstrate resolve and commitment to get the job done. With the wealth of resources at hand, he encourages the necessity to leverage opportunities and resources to achieve both personal and communal success and channel our efforts and time in meaningful ways to empower our communities. In his chapter, Keon will chronicle his personal story and identify specific tools and skills young men have at hand, not only to become individuals of influence, but to make lasting impacts whereby they leave a legacy through harnessing their potential.

On a personal note, Keon is married to his wife Kishauna for almost three years. He is an avid Los Angeles Lakers and Bayern Munich fan. In addition, he is a Youth Leader and relishes traveling to meet new people and experience the different flavors of culture.

Personal Profile

Key Words

Action, Character, Consistency, Potential, Transcendent

Favorite Quote

"The heights by great men reached and kept were not attained by sudden flight, but they, while their companions slept, were toiling upward in the night." ~ Henry Wadsworth Longfellow

Values

Family, Community Enrichment, Youth Empowerment, Financial Freedom, Personal Development

Marketable Skills

Mentorship/Leadership
Networking
Professional Development
Proposal/Project Management
Public Speaking

Contact Information

Website – www.keonreid.com

Email – keon.reid@alumni.emory.edu

LinkedIn – https://www.linkedin.com/in/keon-reid/

Facebook – https://www.facebook.com/keon.reid1

Instagram – @_keonreid

Twitter – @_keonreid

A WASTED MAN

Keon Reid

Here I am a wasted man searching for what is to be,
Looking in the mirror as the sands of the time flee.
Waiting to see what the next breaths hold,
And foraging life's shadows for my image to mold.

Waste they say, am I they speak of?
Oh, how life a brute one I wish was kinder.
Caught in an endless cycle of a broken system,
Nowhere to go but down, into a place I'm sinking.

But then the beacon of light shines through,
A brother, a father, a friend with truth.
He speaks so bold and with confidence he exudes,
Reminds me of what I also can do.

Wasted many may think and that which I thought too,
But here alas, my hope and life to become anew.
I hear a voice from deep within,
That cries aloud to waste no more; it is a sin.
I am a man with deep roots that no longer grows thin,

Who before was lied to by the reflection that made life so grim.
But now with righteous indignation, I can fight a more.
Welcome young man; you're lost no more!

The mirror that once lied and led me astray,
Is now the one with conviction that brings joy to my day.
I am a man not wasted by the dusk and dawn of day,
Now welcome me; identity found and meaning restored.

A wasted man no more, but one brim with future,
A joy and conviction with meaning of one's great duty.
To all I say a wasted man no more,
I have found myself, this time for sure!

It's hard to stop, reflect and ask yourself, where did I go wrong? Deep within, I was bewildered, yet resigned to the truth. I sat, sunken, holding back the tears and wondered to myself, how had it slipped away? Their stares peered deep into my soul, knocking at the door, asking me to open my ears and accept my pending future for this harsh truth – I was done. Five years went down the drain. Five years I thought wasted away. Five years to be in this seat disillusioned by being so close but not even being able to taste it – my PhD.

It was a wonderful Wednesday afternoon, with perfect autumn weather in October. There was a cool wind and the glory of the bright oranges nestled between the greens and reds of turning leaves. This day in question was another major hurdle to overcome. I was brimming with hope of drawing one-step closer to leaving graduate school. Here sat before me, my graduate committee of world-renowned chemists, men who would evaluate my progress and seal my fate. My presentation was shaky in areas, but I felt confident with the progress I had made in recent months. I had it in the bag. Big mistake! After completing my fifth year report, I sat anxiously outside in the lobby greeting familiar faces while the committee deliberated. This time in particular, the deliberations were taking uncommonly longer than expected. Naturally, I began to pray. Nervousness set in for sure. If God is real, then now is the time to show up big time. My boss called me in and he, along with the committee, expressed that although I produced quality work, my progress was too slow and I hadn't developed some core competencies necessary at that stage of my degree to continue as a PhD candidate. They recommended it best for me to stop here with my Master's degree. Talk about a tough pill to swallow! I mustered up enough energy to thank them for their guidance and help throughout the years. They left me with positive remarks and encouraged me as I prepared to move forward in my future.

This event was a shattering and broken moment in my life. Here I thought I could have done my Master's within a year or two; but in retrospect, it took five whole years. Imagine everyone you know understands you are going for your PhD, and have started calling you "Doc" or "Dr. Reid" and you start getting comfortable with the title. It was almost as if I had gotten there at some points, although I had reservations with people calling me "Doc." This crushing blow was my toughest and I was absolutely mortified. My wife, parents and community of friends all shared the burden of my disappointment. Most were comforting and those closest to me shared some harsh truths. The reality is that I divested my time with other commitments and the fear of failure crippled me from really pushing to learn some fundamental and core principles in my degree. My life had taken a turn and my future direction was unclear. Over the ensuing months, I reflected long and hard about areas I could have improved, studied harder, sought more help, and the works. Eventually, it boiled down to one underlying factor – me.

My reflection left me to believe I was a wasted man, hence the title of this chapter. I assumed my five years in graduate school were wasted; I had wasted my potential. As I transitioned to look for jobs, I had some thought-provoking and meaningful conversations with peers and mentors. One previous advisor noted that I would look back at this time in graduate school and realize it was a blessing in disguise. Another reminded me that I just got a free Master's degree. Hmm, I never thought about it that way. Eventually, it hit me; I was actually done with graduate school. The late nights, the coding, the reading articles, the weekly meetings and presentations were done! This realization sprung more belief and enthusiasm to forge onward. To fast forward, I've had three jobs since graduate school and I now work as a Proposal Manager for the world's largest merchant acquirer and payment processor, First Data. In the past year and a half, there's been many challenges, but on the heel of each other, a new opportunity emerged. Through faith in God and resiliency to fight on, I am unraveling my identity and resolved that I am not a wasted man – there is untapped potential that I am now realizing.

To my brothers, the choices you have made or the countless mistakes you hold onto are not indicative of who you are. A *Wasted Man* is not someone who has lost hope or missed the mark in realizing who he is; instead, a *Wasted Man* is the acknowledgment that the world has not encountered the *real* you. You have boundless potential that, once activated, will bring change to your families and community. One must note that to emerge as a leader, change agent, catalyst, philanthropist or millionaire, it requires work. My charge is that as you read this chapter, you are compelled to first evaluate and reflect on who you are and once your truth is identified, you mobilize to empower and develop yourself. The world needs you and as such, you cannot sit idly and forego the purpose and true meaning of your life. Value is found when your worth impacts another life. Therefore, a "Wasted Man" must **A.C.T.** First, a *Wasted Man* must **take action** to find meaning in one's self and work arduously to realize his purpose and effect change. Second, a *Wasted Man* must **work towards consistency,** as this is the breeding ground for excellence. Third, a *Wasted Man* must endeavor to **become transcendent** in his field of influence.

Action

Henry Wadsworth Longfellow stated, "The heights by great men reached and kept were not attained by sudden flight, but they, while their companions slept, were toiling upward in the night." This has been my favorite quote for almost two decades. I was careful to note that the first thing required of us as men is to take action in work. Longfellow taught me a keen lesson as a boy. To become a great man, it requires sacrifice through action. We all have dreams of being rich or living truly contented lives, but few arrive to this achievement. The words that speak volumes in Longfellow's quote are "reached," "kept," "toiling" and "upward." As a man, I have learned that nothing really comes easily. You have to work hard for it. Sometimes, we work amiss, for example with my PhD. Nevertheless, there is hope because we consistently have the opportunity to get back up and try again.

Growing up as a child in Jamaica, I had big dreams to be a bus conductor, before my mother rubbished that thought quickly. There was a pure exhilaration in how the conductors drew the crowds, the brute yet suave tone they had to sway people from other taxis or buses. The ones that were most successful had a loud cadence, were eager to spot someone needing a ride and swift to aid the person to get on the bus. They were filled with energy and did their jobs with confidence and apt persuasion. Although my mother swayed me to pursue more secure professions, there were somethings I captured from their value and work ethic that we as men should have. Irrespective of our positions or fields of influence in life, it is important to show up and give your best effort. You must have goals, intent and the willpower to do everything legally possible to get the job done. There were times I jumped on a bus and it was a small crowd, but in a matter of about 15 minutes, we would have 20 plus people seated and headed towards work or school. An honest work is to be commended, so whether you are picking up trash or you are the CEO, it all requires the same thing – action.

What is the enemy of action? It is inaction. Working towards goals is easier said than done. We must be cognizant that life requires a delicate work-life balance. By neglecting responsibilities or not strategically implementing targets and deadlines, we run the risk of working aimlessly, being burnt out and wasting our time. We can combat inaction by keeping calendars, becoming accountable to others and constantly evaluating our efforts against our goals.

Consistency

Consistency and zeal will accomplish what zeal alone cannot do. One's success relies less on luck and more on consistency. As men, we are typically single-threaded thinkers, but lack the principle of critical reflection or evaluation. Consistency is an anchor that yields results when action or zeal for something dies away. Often, I have the impetus to tackle new projects, read new books or learn a new skill; but each project is soon forgotten because the eagerness, which birthed the idea to tackle the project, soon burns out. How many times have you had a big dream? How many times have you had that million-dollar idea? How many times did you make a decision to quit a bad habit? Yes, it is more times than we would like to count. The truth stems from us not taking action nor following through with being consistent. We need to find a driving force to fuel our consistency; for me, that is Jesus Christ. My faith, coupled with a personal drive for success, is a commonality that pushes me to be consistent and strive for greatness.

Consistency governs achievement. As a man, you cannot neglect this truth. It allows you to measure your goals and track progress, not to mention it allows you to maintain an ethical message. Moreover, consistency makes you relevant creating accountability to establish your reputation. Iconic figures such as Jesus Christ, Mahatma Gandhi, Bob Marley, Kobe Bryant and may I even argue Adolf Hitler, were solidified in the history books because of their influence, governed by years of consistency. My last example should be alarming to you. Consistency can be related either to something good or bad. Our understanding should be that it is a dangerous weapon and when tooled for the wrong purpose, it will yield deadly results, the most gruesome being the death of millions of lives.

It is undeniably clear that consistency can be a two-edged sword and I have witnessed this issue in my own life. Back in my undergraduate days, I loved playing FIFA, the soccer game on Xbox. I invested many years and hours into playing this video game to the point that I was ranked in the top five percent across the world! Mind you, millions of people buy and play FIFA annually. Looking back, there were definitely other ways I could have spent my time. My consistency and dedication elevated me to be one of the best in the world. On the contrary, I was working multiple jobs, doing research and did not commit enough time to

104

my coursework. I struggled in some of my courses as a result and failed some exams. The lack of preparation and studying produced failing grades. In the same way, the lack of action and consistency will lead to failure across different areas in your life. After seeing the negative correlation, I scaled back on my extracurricular activities, FIFA, and sought help through tutors and study groups. What became evident was that I had consistency in an area of my life that was not important in my progression as a college student. It leads me to believe that consistency must be coupled with focus and priority. My newfound consistency and effort yielded passing grades; and in the end, I graduated magna cum laude. Men should have clearly defined goals and evaluation. Too often, we work without seeing the results of our efforts. Society enforces a culture where men should be the breadwinner, but far too often, that comes to the detriment of emotional and spiritual edification of our families. Our women need us fully engaged to act as fathers, brothers and sons; therefore, we need to develop consistency to show up to kids' activities, game nights, date nights and in our churches and communities.

What is the enemy of consistency? It is inconsistency. Consistency develops core competencies such as perseverance, discipline, integrity and diligence in the face of insurmountable challenges. As we reflect and begin to map our lives, we have to acknowledge that a *Wasted Man* must overcome his inconsistencies because it is key to realizing his true identity. In our personal lives, we have to dig to find meaning in our value and exercise that truth.

Transcendent

A transcendent man is one who leaves an indelible imprint on society or lives he touches. A man who is transcendent has taken action to steadily and consistently work at a goal for the betterment of others. Each man has the innate ability to be transcendent, but one can be a *Wasted Man* should he not take arm to work for the betterment of others. Damian Marley, Bob Marley's son, stated, "We sent man to the moon, yet we can't solve crime and poverty." It was eight years after President John F. Kennedy announced a national plan to send man to the moon that the Apollo 11 completed its mission. That took 2,974 days, $25.4 billion dollars and dedicated individuals to accomplish one of the greatest feats in history. Armstrong famously stated after taking his first step, "That's one small step for man, one giant leap for mankind." His quote almost simplifies the gravity of effort it took to land man on the moon and return him to Earth safely.

Not to minimize this remarkable accomplishment, but how beneficial was that to mankind? Marley's statement on crime and poverty alludes to a far greater social concern gone largely unaddressed, albeit crime and poverty are endemic worldwide due to sin and other factors. People are largely aware of the issue, but only a few venture to change it. In Matthew 25, Jesus delineates a goat from sheep by drawing parallel to helping those in need. A goat he describes as one who doesn't help the sick, feed the hungry or visit someone in prison, whereas the sheep is a person that tends to those in need. In reality, we as men naturally want to be goats. We have our own affairs to address and relinquish the responsibility to another man or woman to get the job. However, today I am calling for us to be sheep, to walk in humility and serve for the better good of our families and communities. Beyond areas of concern in the global affairs, there are areas in which we as men have failed to be transcendent, areas in which we have failed to go above and beyond the call of duty. The goal in manhood is to be a life-giving source to his community. This change starts first with your home, then to your community and finally to your world. We are men who can champion influence in our societies, effect change and be men above reproach, men with good character and men of excellence.

What is the enemy of transcendence? It is failure to act and follow through. Those who have left an indelible mark on humanity came from a conviction that prompted action and was governed in consistency. A man who surpasses the ordinary can become exceptional. If you continue to be exceptional, you can become transcendent. Every man can become transcendent in his own essence. The Nobel Prize and Lifetime Achievement awards are two notable areas of recognition for a body of work. They encapsulate what it means to **A.C.T.** Recognition is a byproduct of someone who truly is transcendent, but it is important to note that not every transcendent man is recognized in a profound way. There are men who are silent rivers – they run deep – their influence is far reaching, yet it is not publicized. We must be careful not to be proud rather we should walk in humility and be patient in our efforts. Those who are transcendent walk the long road less traveled by other men. Robert Frost, in his poem *The Road Not Taken,* identifies the road less travelled as the one "that has made all the difference." My hope is that we load a caravan of men whose perspective changes about being a *Wasted Man*. My prayer is that we realize the potential we have inside of us, and use the support we have through brotherhood to magnify what it means to be a man. You are the man to make the difference.

A Wasted Man No More

As a little boy, I enjoyed selling and helping in my grandmother's community grocery shop. One of my fondest memories was personally buying or selling the balloons that came in an assortment. The grid was numbered from 1 to 100 and you had to choose a number for your purchase. I remember squeezing the neck of the balloon and loving that high-pitched squealing that annoyed everyone, but it was pure amusement for me. What I found interesting was the variety of sizes, shapes, colors and types of balloons that came in the assortment. I was mad when I bought a baby balloon and always laughed uncontrollably when others got it. You know how boys are; we use every opportunity to troll and have humor at others' expense. My true excitement came when I got a big balloon! It meant a lot to know that my balloon was the biggest and at that time, bigger was always better. It wasn't until much later in life that I began to have greater appreciation for the value and lessons I could learn from a balloon. Balloons are diverse in their nature and purposes, and similarly are the potential and purposes of men. It is a splendor to see both balloons and men truly fulfill their purpose.

Although somewhat simple of an illustration, I do believe it is fitting to talk about a balloon's nature and how it relates to your life. If you would, follow me in your mind's eye. Hold out your hand and open your palm. Here, in your hand, you have an uninflated balloon. You can imagine what color, size or shape it is – this balloon represents you! If you were to put the balloon at your mouth and blow, it would fill with air and once it seems to be at full capacity, you stop. Tie your balloon. In your hand, you now have a filled balloon. What you just did demonstrates the transition from a *Wasted Man* to one who maximizes his potential and now serves a richer purpose. Now, let it go. What happened? That's right! It fell to the ground. To get the balloon filled, it required action in the form of firm, consistent blowing. However, once you were finished and let it go, it fell to the ground. Many of us can work hard for a long time without truly seeing the rewards of our efforts.

Let me introduce another method – the element helium. Balloons have the ability to float when filled with helium gas because it is lighter than air. Without anything holding it, it will float off into the sky. I liken filling your balloon with helium to being transcendent and being filled with God's Holy Spirit. Unlike filling the balloon with your own flawed air that sinks, God's perfect air allows one to become transcendent. Helium is like Jesus Christ in that once He is in our lives, He lifts us beyond our circumstance and takes us higher and makes us greater. Without Jesus Christ, men sink and become the lowest common denominator. I believe He is the only one that can truly make men transcendent. Similar to the Apollo 11 being launched, any balloon that begins to soar in the air immediately captures the attention of all to behold – whether it is the child who lost the balloon by accident and stands there crying hoping it returns, or the parent chuckling and looking up saying to themselves, there's no way for me to get that. Transcendence gives greater value to who you are and in the areas that you serve. You can be a single father or the head of a multinational corporation. Jesus enables us to be influencers and transformative figures in the world through our own special way.

Each man has limitless purpose, but it is tied to our identity. As you look at that balloon, what does it look like? Who are you? Your brother cannot help you identify your true identity. Your identity is most complete when filled with Christ. A *Wasted Man* must **A.C.T.** If we return to the opening poem, I discussed looking in the mirror. Knowing who you are in Christ is the key to becoming transcendent. As men, we must reflect to challenge our fears and doubt. More importantly, reflection allows us to come to grips with who we truly are by identifying our purpose. As men, let us stand together and help each other to understand and maximize our potential. Start today by making the decision that you will be a *Wasted Man* no more!

~Dedication~

To be honest, I don't have enough space for my dedication; I have been blessed to have rich connections to so many men who have supported me throughout my life. First, I am eternally grateful for my dad, Henrick Reid. His sacrifice, encouragement and love are principles I strive to emulate daily. My pastor, Apostle Devon Swaby, has provided keen guidance for over a decade, of which I am truly thankful. Additionally, I inherited a new father in Ian McDonald through marriage. He is a man of prayer, principle and ethics. In all, I have a triumvirate of influential fathers who continue to shape who I am. My grandfathers and uncles have equally shared the responsibility of nurturing me. I'd like to especially say thank you to my grandfathers, Jasper Brown and Cyrus "Papa" Reid. Great men are born of great men.

In addition to my fatherly guidance, God has been kind to give me true brothers who have encouraged and stood beside me in various facets. To you all, this chapter is a culmination of your strong influences on my life:

- *Andre Ashley*
- *Andrew "Granty or DJ Bag Juice" Grant*
- *Bishop "Bre" Herrington*
- *Daniel Porter*
- *Easton "Jegge or East" Grant*
- *Jamal "Jammy" Davis*
- *Keith "Kap Beatz" Phillip*
- *Nickoy "Captain" Campbell*

- *Phillip "Prezzi" Grant*
- *Riann Reid*
- *Stephen Cunningham*

Finally, I would be remiss if I did not acknowledge my mentors and coaches. Not only are they experts in their field, they continue to provide the sound advice needed to realize my potential. To a few of my special mentors, thank you!

- *Dr. Davon Kennedy*
- *Dr. Donald Hamelberg*
- *Dr. James Kindt*
- *Thomas Mercer*
- *Thomas Scott*

Biography of Elder Ronald Rice

Elder Ronald Rice has a tremendous passion for preaching the Word of God to a lost and dying world. He was born in Seaside, California to Ronald F. Rice, Sr. and Dorothy C. Rice in 1975. A few years after moving to Durham, N.C. in 1976 with his family, they began to attend Mt. Zion Baptist Church, under the leadership of the Reverend Donald Q. Fozard, Sr.

From the young age of twelve, Elder Rice was born again, water baptized, and filled with the Holy Ghost. The Lord had put it in his heart that he would one day preach the gospel of Jesus Christ, which was later confirmed in prophecy by many men of God. After giving in to peer-pressure and the cares of this world over the years, "Ronnie," his nickname, walked away from the things of God and began to embark on a path of destruction, which he would later regret. Sin almost pushed him over the edge with depression and into suicide, but he called on the Lord and was delivered at the age of twenty-three while finishing school at North Carolina State University. Ever since, he has been on fire for the Lord, returning to Mt. Zion Christian Church under the leadership of Apostle Donald Q. Fozard, Sr.

He resides there as an Elder, Sunday School teacher, Street Evangelist and Youth Pastor. Evangelist Rice is currently pursuing his Master of Divinity degree from Hosanna Bible College in Durham, N.C. He also teaches Bible and Spanish at Mt. Zion Christian Academy in Durham, N.C. He preaches holiness, and demonstrates the love of God through signs and wonders. He has

113

been married to the former Christa L. Wilcox for 20 years, and they have four children, all of whom are active in the ministry. Evangelist Rice maintains a standard to keep and God to glorify.

Personal Profile

Key Words

Evangelize, Inspire, Reach, Teach, Exemplify

Favorite Quote

"Your ability to succeed is dependent upon your thoughts in life."

Values

Compassionate, Futuristic Thinking, Creative, Humility

Marketable Skills

Public Speaking, Leading, Bilingual, Lifelong Student

Contact Information

Email: ronald.rice@mzcadurham.org

Facebook Profile: Evangelist Ron Rice

LinkedIn Profile: Elder Ronald Rice

BEING A GODLY MAN IN AN UNGODLY WORLD

Elder Ronald Rice

Before we dive into the subject, I want you men to know a little more about me. I was raised in the church, and born again at the age of 12. I made a vow that my life would be sold out for Christ. As I got older, I fell into the trap that many young men experience. My friends began to add to their habits of playing video games to also playing girls. They were all around and giving me attention and I began to fall into the trap of the enemy. Sex, drugs, and perversion replaced the holy living and vow that I made to God. After finishing high school, I continued on this track at North Carolina State University in Raleigh, NC. The Lord kept sending young men to minister to me and remind me of my promised commitment to Him, but I kept on ignoring them and doing what I thought was my own thing. On the outside, I seemed to be having the time of my life, partying, hanging out with the boys, traveling, etc., but I was empty inside. It grew to a place where I became depressed. My thoughts were never to kill myself physically, but my mindset was, "If I catch a disease like AIDS or HIV, I really don't even care because I don't even love my life!" I met someone who I felt would bring me joy, but the emptiness continued to grow, even though I settled down with one girl. We were together for almost two years, and I heard some news that shook me. It made me think that my life was actually over. I found out that a young lady that I slept with had died of AIDS. After being tested and rehearsing over all the girls, I had been with in my mind, my fear of death escalated. The devil tormented me day and night, reminding me of what I said in my despair. I cried out to God and said, "God, if You save me from this, I will live for You the rest of my life!" After two grueling weeks of waiting on the results, I found out that I was disease free. The rest is history. I rededicated my life to Christ, married my girlfriend, and have been living for God for the past 21 years. The Scriptures that I am using are the ones that I applied to my life and saw the power of God move in me tremendously. I'm not just preaching to you based on what the Word of God says, but also from daily application of it to my life. I pray that what is shared will bless your life and help you in your walk with the Lord.

This world is a very beautiful place. When you look at the landmarks such as the oceans, mountain ranges, grasslands, along with the buildings, streets, and houses that man has built, they all make this earth breathtaking at times. From a spiritual and moral perspective however, you will get a very different experience. Corruption from the highest offices all the way down to the law enforcement (who is supposed to "protect and serve") is prevalent. Evil thoughts and actions dominate the headlines, and sin seems to be on the mind of every other person you meet. All types of sex, lies, and crime are in just about everything that comes on the "hellavision." Society is becoming more "in your face" by consistently revealing things that should be sacred and inappropriate for the general public. The devil seems to be executing his plan to steal, kill, and destroy mankind to perfection.

Many people, including naive Christians are falling to his attacks and schemes due to their ignorance of his devices (2 Corinthians 2:11). So how do we as men keep God first and escape the corruption that is in this world through lust (2 Peter 1:4)? Our answer is faith in the Word of God and prayer. In this chapter, we will draw our thoughts from 1 Peter 3:10-12, and elaborate on the instructions (in bold).

1 Peter 3:10-12 *For he that will love life, and see good days, let him refrain his tongue from evil, and his lips that they speak no guile: 11 let him eschew evil, and do good; let him seek peace, and ensue it. 12 For the eyes of the Lord are over the righteous, and his ears are open unto their prayers: but the face of the Lord is against them that do evil.*

Tongue Control

Proverbs 13:3 *He that keepeth his mouth keepeth his life: but he that openeth wide his lips shall have destruction.*

When God tells us to refrain our tongues from evil, He means all manner of evil. Evil simply means unmoral, sinful, or wicked. It means that anything I associate myself with that is causing my tongue to say evil things is evil. One of the areas that many young men have allowed their tongues to speak evil is in the area of secular music. We have to understand that music of the world is "demonic," and is contrary to the way a man of God should speak. It is full of lust, profanity, perversion, and satanic symbolism. The Word of God tells us not to fellowship with the "unfruitful works of darkness" (Ephesians 5:11). In other words, if I really love God as much as I say that I do, and really want to enjoy my life, I will obey Him and fill myself with His Word.

Proverbs 18:21 *Death and life are in the power of the tongue: and they that love it shall eat the fruit thereof.*

Many of us don't equate negative speaking as evil, but it is. God's Word emphasizes that we keep evil speaking out of our mouths. He tells us to be slow to speak (James 1:19). How many times have we said things that we really didn't mean because of pressure, anger, etc.? We have to choose our words carefully that we allow to come out of our mouths because they carry the power to bring life or death to a situation. Whether we realize it or not, our words shape our lives. That is why it's so important to speak the Word of God over our own lives, families, and friends so that His will for us can be experienced. Are there times in our lives when things don't go as planned? Of course! As long as Satan is around doing what he does best, we are going to have conflict and evil days that can shake our foundations to the core, (if we let it)! As I'm writing this chapter, my family is in the midst of an attack that has escalated into a health situation for my wife. Her body has been attacked with sickness that the doctors have said that it is chronic (no cure). As a man of faith and preacher of God's Word, daily I look right into the face of a helpless situation (in the natural) and speak the Word of life into her. No matter what it looks like, I refuse to let my tongue speak evil! The healing of her body *will* manifest, because a supernatural word spoken in faith *always* causes a natural situation to line up with it. I have seen the power of God heal many people that I have prayed for, and this situation is nothing for God to turn around! As long as I continue to speak life, the prayer of faith will save her and the Lord will raise her up (James 5:15)!

Our Lips Shouldn't Speak Deceitfully

Matthew 5:37 *But let your communication be, Yea, yea; Nay, nay: for whatsoever is more than these cometh of evil.*

Let's take a look at the following Scriptures…

Matthew 15:8-9 *This people draweth nigh unto me with their mouth, and honoureth me with their lips; but their heart is far from me. 9 But in vain they do worship me, teaching for doctrines the commandments of men.*

Our worship to God is deceitful and vain if He doesn't have our heart. This reminds me of many times in my life when I spoke things deceitfully just to get what I wanted. How many of you fellas have said to females, "I love you," just to get some action? Or better yet, made a promise to someone to get out of a current dilemma that you know you weren't going to keep? Anytime we say or do things to get a desired reaction out of a person when we really don't have the other person's interest at heart is deceitful. If we tell the Lord that we love Him and express gratitude through our lips, but our life actions are full of sin, we have spoken deceitfully to Him. Moreover, He already knows it anyway. Love is more than talk; it is action. The devil is the master of deceit. His temptation aroused Adam and Eve's attention by convincing them that they were missing something, but his plan was motivated by deception and greed. The results had harsh consequences, which still has a lasting effect on all mankind. As a man, how can I avoid being deceitful? The answer is simple… Say what you mean, and mean what you say.

Avoid Evil and Do Good

1 Thessalonians 5:22 *Abstain from all appearance of evil.*

In the first part of the chapter, we saw how God commands us to stop speaking evil. This part focuses on avoiding evil all together. How can evil be avoided when it is all around us? Some situations can't be avoided, but just because there is evil all around men, it doesn't mean that I have to participate in it. If you can control it, avoid it. 1 Corinthians 15:33 says, *"Be not deceived: evil communication corrupts good manners."* For example, when I was growing up, some of my friends used to smoke weed. When they got ready to smoke, I would step out of the car because I didn't want to smoke or smell like it. After many months of watching them smoke, laugh uncontrollably, and get the "munchies," my desire increased to want and try it. It seemed as if I was missing a lot of the so-called fun, and eventually I gave in and started smoking with them. The point of the story is the evil association that I chose to stay around caused my good behavior to become corrupted, which led to a downward spiral of my character and the formation of other bad habits.

On one end, God tells us to stay away from evil situations. On the other hand, He tells us to do good. 1 John 3:7 says, *"Little children, let no man deceive you: he that doeth righteousness is righteous, even as He is righteous."* Sometimes as men, we forget that God is our Father, and that His Word is instructions to His children. In order to please Him, we must obey Him. We can't make excuses for our repeated wrongdoings. 1 John 1:9 says that, *if we confess our sins, He is faithful and just to forgive us our sins, and to cleanse us of all unrighteousness.* In other words, if we are sincere and honest with God about our sin, He forgives and cleanses us. We then show our gratitude to God for the act of mercy that we have shown, and separate ourselves from the situations that caused us to disappoint our Father.

It is much easier to do good when you see what God does for those who are obedient to Him. Better yet, in every aspect of life, whether it is a childhood or adult choice, the people who obey instructions are the most successful people. The men who stay out of trouble and do the right things have a higher chance of success than those who do not.

Seek Peace and Follow It

Isaiah 26:3 *Thou wilt keep him in perfect peace, whose mind is stayed on thee: because he trusteth in thee.*

Jesus said in John 14:27, *"Peace I leave with you, my peace I give unto you: not as the world giveth, give I unto you. Let not your heart be troubled, neither let it be afraid."* God's peace cannot be explained. It is an overwhelming confidence that causes us not to worry about anything. Peace is something God freely gives to anyone who receives Him. The world constantly searches for ways to bring peace to the earth, not realizing that God sent the Prince of Peace and solved that problem long ago. I'm going to address peace from two different standpoints: inner and outer peace.

Inner Peace

The Word of God tells us that God's peace that "passes all understanding, will keep our hearts and minds through Christ Jesus" (Philippians 4:7). His peace is designed to keep us sane in an insane world. No matter what trial, test, or circumstance that comes our way, He promises to keep us in peace. How is that possible? By faith! We have to stay in faith, walk by faith, live by faith, speak faith, and work our faith. In the same chapter of Philippians, verse 9, the Scripture tells us to do the things we have learned, received, heard and seen in God, and His peace will be with us.

Peace is also one of the fruit of the Spirit listed in Galatians 5:22. It is part of the character of God that He demands us to walk in (Galatians 5:25). When tragedy strikes or we receive a bad report, God's peace will bring calmness to our hearts and minds. We have to remember that nothing catches our Father by surprise, and all things work together for good to them that love Him (Romans 8:28). He still speaks to us and lets us know that everything is okay, even in the midst of chaos. Many things happen in life that we will not truly understand, but we still have to trust God and know that He is our refuge and draw strength from Him. Having a peace of mind doesn't mean that we aren't going to ever get emotional, but the Word will still be spoken. The peace that we have in God produces a type of unshakable confidence that reminds us of how big God is and His ability to make the impossible possible. It also demonstrates that He is the only one that can truly console and help us in our "evil day," and our times of grieving and disappointments in life.

Outer Peace

Romans 12:18 *If it be possible, as much as lieth in you, live peaceably with all men.*

If you really think about it, walking in peace with God is easy. No matter how much we are disobedient or come short of His expectations, He still forgives us. The challenging part at times in our lives is getting along with other men, and forgiving them for wronging us. Mankind in general is not as forgiving as God is. We have a tendency to hold grudges and be vindictive at times.

Many of us men are victims of things that seem unforgivable, and it's hard to let that stuff go. How do we get past these things in our lives? Jesus addressed these points in His teaching on unforgiveness. In Mark 11:25-26, He said that when we go to God in prayer, we must forgive if we are holding anything against anyone. If we don't, He will not forgive us. If we expect God to forgive us of all the times we have lied to Him, cursed Him, disobeyed Him, etc., He expects us to do the same. Many times in my life I promised God I was going [and never going] to do something, only to end up breaking my word. He still forgave me, without ever bringing up anything I have done in my past! With His Spirit inside of us, He commands us to be as forgiving as He is. Sometimes it's tough to forgive, especially when our manhood is challenged. That's why the majority of this chapter is laced with Scriptures. When we take them off the page and apply them to our lives, we will see God's power in our lives!

The second point that Jesus made in the Word concerning forgiveness is when the disciples asked, "How many times should I forgive my brother when he sins against me" (Matthew 18:21-22)? He responded by telling them to forgive seventy times seven; 490 times, which is unlimited! Personally, if someone sinned against me this much, I would have to find another environment to be in. What can we do if we have someone in our life that has wronged us, or is continually lying on you and/or talking evil about you? Jesus tells us to pray for those that "despitefully use you and persecute you" (Matthew 5:44). I used to say that this is "easier said than done," but I realized that when you pray for your enemies, it's hard to stay mad at them. In prayer, God will show you the spirit that is in operation, and when you come against that spirit, you're addressing the real problem. Our fight isn't against each other, but against the influence of the spirit causing them to do hateful things against you. Men that are living for the devil are influenced by the devil, and vice versa. We don't influence our own selves or generate our own nature. Once I understood this, it made dealing with all types of people easier. Sometimes I still forget this and get confrontational, but the Spirit of God will "check" me and show what spirit is in operation, prompting me to go into warfare in the spirit.

I want to leave you men of God with two Scriptures that can be vital for success in our lives…

1 Thessalonians 5:17 *Pray without ceasing.*

1 Peter 2:17 *Honor all men.* ***Love the brotherhood****. Fear God. Honor the king.*

As we stay in prayer daily and consistently, our attitude towards men will be love, honor and respect. Our reverence of God will cause us to be examples to the ones that do not know Him, and we will be witnesses of His glory in our lives. I appreciate the chance to speak encouraging words into your hearts and I pray that you will be blessed and prosperous, and fulfill every dream and vision that God has placed in your lives. If you obey the instructions, God will allow you to spend your days in prosperity, and your years in pleasures (Job 36:11). Just don't give up and give in to the temptations of the world. It is truly a walk of faith and patience, but it pays off in the end! Much love to you brothers!

~Dedication~

I would like to dedicate this chapter to my son Nehemiah Rice, the students (former and active) at Mount Zion Christian Academy, the young men (former and active participants) in our youth ministry, and the players that I have coached while I was a coach (too many people to name). I would also like to dedicate this chapter to the men who I have worked with in ministry, and will read this book because their lives will be changed.

Biography of Todd Rose

Todd Rose, entrepreneur, author, and businessman, are three words that describe what Tod Sterling Rose does. However, the words father, husband and overall student of life would encompass who he is.

Rose is a 1997 graduate of the historic Morris Brown College in Atlanta, GA. where he earned a bachelor's degree in Journalism. As an entrepreneur, Rose owns T.S. Rose Enterprises, LLC that is comprised of two distinct, yet related businesses: copycontentarticles.com and budgetsearchpro.com. Through these entities, he employs his expert internet marketing skills to help other entrepreneurs' market and grow their businesses online and he lends his talents as a copywriter and ghostwriter to help clients from range of industries find their brand and storytelling voices.

As a father and husband, his greatest joys are being a faithful loving husband to his wife LaKimbriea and father to his four children, Tiana (8), Catherine (18), Malik (21) and Jarell (23). As an author, he has ghostwritten two books and is working on several projects including an autobiography examining his personal spiritual journey and a book outlining his experiences as a non-custodial parent. Rose credits his early upbringing in a military family growing up in Ansbach, Germany from age five to age 11 as one of his most endearing lifelong gifts.

While overseas, he encountered a plethora of cultures, people and experiences that shaped his world-view at a young age and allowed his consciousness to transcend the trivialities of race, religion, prejudice and negative societal constructs that infect the minds of men and plague humanity. He says his diverse childhood has perpetually enlightened his spiritual journey and ignited his soul with a humble flame of purpose. Ultimately, he understands he is an earthly vessel of the most high designed to fulfill a mission as G.O.D., Generator, Operator and Director of a divine purpose.

Personal Profile

Key Words

1. Godly
2. Invictus
3. Triumphant
4. Perseverance
5. Committed

Favorite Quote

"I am G.O.D., the Generator, Operator & Director of my destiny."
~ Todd Rose

Values

Family, Leadership, Responsibility, Personal Transformation, Mutual Respect, Inner Vision, the Ability and Capacity to Dream, Succeed & Prosper

Marketable Skill

Copywriting & Editing, Digital Marketing Expertise, Public Speaking, Public Relations

Contact Information

Email: todsrose@gmail.com

Phone: (678) 634-1448

Website: todsrose.com

Search Services: budgetsearchpro.com

Writing Services: copycontentarticles.com

MANHOOD UNDER SIEGE: PUTTING THE "MAN" BACK IN MANHOOD

Todd Rose

W hen first hearing the phrase, *Men Magnifying Manhood* my initial thought was that, no mission could be timelier. My second thought was a "thank you" to the Most High for the opportunity to lend my time, talents and experiences to this highly valued and worthwhile discussion. It is with heart-felt soul-deep gratitude, humility and purpose that I share my personal testimony in the hopes that it may ignite a positive thought; an insightful inspiration; or an identifiable course-correction or affirmation in the earthly path of a young man walking the path I once walked. May it help lead one whom is lost in the world from estray to a closer walk with the godly man that resides within. In the spirit of healing and fortifying the true purpose of the male principle, I offer my mistakes, my revelations, and my salvation.

Two Crucial Mistakes - When I was a child, I thought as a child ...

I became a father in 1996 at the age of 24, long before I was truly ready to be one. At that age, I was like most men, merely a big boy with manly organs lacking the mental capacity to understand the gift and responsibility that God had bestowed upon me being born a male and being a father. I was handsome, intelligent, and ambitious but also lustful and reckless; a dangerous combination as it were. I was at the top of my game riding high on the wave of popularity that came with joining one of the most popular fraternities on the campus of one of Atlanta's most coveted HBCUs. In many ways, I felt I had escaped becoming one of the proverbial 24-year-old statistics destined to ride the pipeline-to-prison. By all accounts, I was successful and destined for even more success. However, I didn't fully understand the principles of manhood, even though I was in the body of a full-grown male. I felt I could do no wrong and that I was God's gift to any woman lucky enough to become one of my conquests. With the ratio of 13 women to every one man on campus, drunken one-night-stands were a routine. It wasn't long before a lust-filled night of pleasure resulted in a young lady, who I barely knew, becoming pregnant with my child before either of us were ready to be parents. At that point, my life took a turn down a course that I would spend the next two decades trying to understand and correct. In my childish mind, I chose to ignore the situation having received no "official" word from the young lady. In my mind, it didn't happen and I just continued to live my carefree life not realizing the true impact of my actions; on both my son's mother and on my son.

It wasn't until about 18 months later that I found out I had a son by way of a court summons ordering me to submit to a paternity test. Weeks after the test, even after reading the "99.9%

chance that you are the father" of the child on the official letter informing me of the results, I was still partially in denial and haphazardly approached taking responsibility. Despite the evidence, I couldn't wrap my childish mind around being a father. Even after being ordered to pay child support although I had no job and was still a full-time student. I recall being stunned as I left the courthouse that day feeling demeaned and emasculated as if I had just been manhandled with no control over the situation. Still in my selfish immature mind, I was in denial of my responsibility and full of resentment for my son's mother, the court system and myself. I was *not yet thinking like a man.*

In the end, it would take four long years filled with arguments back and forth with my son's mother, receiving nasty letters, missed child support payments and failed half-hearted (and sometimes sabotaged) attempts at visitations with my son to finally wake up and come to grips with my responsibility. By this time, it was 1999 and some progress had been made in the situation with my son who was now six-years-old. We had met and would talk on the phone regularly as we established a bond. I had stepped up to the plate in terms of my status as a father and I had finally graduated from college a couple of years earlier. I was working at a local restaurant while looking for a job in my field of journalism. While there, I had fallen back into using marijuana and selling it to my coworkers to make extra money. I even started actively using cocaine.

Around that time, I also met a young lady working at the restaurant with whom I had a lot in common and we became close. In some ways, manhood began to take hold in my life. But In other ways, vestiges of my childish mentality were still present in my actions. Although I was actively stepping into my fatherly responsibilities, I didn't realize the magnitude of the gamble I was taking with my life selling and using drugs, thus the life of my son

132

whom I was just beginning to really know. Then one night during a dope and alcohol induced stupor, I received a powerful vision of my mature and angry son visiting me in prison. The sheer realness of it shook me to sobriety and I vowed in that moment to never let that vision become a reality and that I would do whatever it took to right the situation. Within a month, I stopped using dope, and got a job as reporter at my hometown newspaper and I moved back home to South Georgia to begin my professional career as a reporter. At that time, I had become very close very quickly with a young lady I met at the restaurant and ***against my better judgement,*** (to the tune of her pleading to come with me as an escape from her estranged relationship with her mother) I changed my stance and I allowed her to move with me. Within a year, we were pregnant, and my precious beautiful daughter was born nine-months later, on December 22, 2000, two days after my birthday. It was an exciting time and we were discussing marriage.

I looked forward to finally being the father I always wanted to be; present, available, hands on, with a measure of control and no distance between us as opposed to the situation with my first child. We were working together to raise our daughter and things appeared fine for a time. However, suddenly, things began to derail. She lost two jobs within months of one another and I noticed her knack for throwing me under the bus each time she spoke with her mother. I soon realized her true level of maturity and her heavy dependence on her mother's opinions, particularly about me. Then one day, unexpectedly, she announced to me how much she hated my hometown and that she planned to take an office manager position in her mother's counseling practice, 4-hours away on the outskirts of Atlanta. My feet must have sunk a full inch into the carpet under the gravity of this news. Yet, she sold it to me as a way to improve our lives together even though I had just transitioned to a local government job at the local health department that payed double what I had made as a reporter.

"I'll bring her down here to see you," she said. Suddenly I felt trapped, hamstringed, hoodwinked, bamboozled and taken advantage of all in one swirling emotion. The realization of the bad choice I had made in a mate was unsettling to say the least but paled compared to the feeling of having to separate from my baby girl under such circumstances. It was gut wrenching and worse still, according to Georgia law. I was powerless to stop her. Once again, I felt emasculated. Yet, I remained calm and out of love. I vowed to transition to an Atlanta-based position within a year to not be away from my daughter any longer than was necessary. Within nine-months, I was hired at the state health department and moved to Atlanta into a home that she was renting (with her mother as a cosigner) that happened to be located next door to her mother. On one hand, my daughter and I were ecstatic about being together again; however, my daughter's mother was not as enthusiastic.

Barely four months after I moved in, over the course of a single weekend church retreat my daughter's mother attended, the entire situation crumbled before my eyes. The day she returned from the church retreat, I grew devil horns and since we were living in sin, I had to move out. A week later, I packed up my stuff, wrote her a check for $300 dollars for support of my daughter and I moved into an extended stay hotel. Ironically, it was the same hotel she was living in when we met after she moved out of her mother's house. And, to add insult to injury, she filed for child support a few months later even though I was already paying. Since she worked for her mother, they cooked the books and made it appear as though she had little to no income. Just like that, another $200 was added to the $300 I was already paying. Again, the irony reared its ugly head. This life lesson was delivered hard, fast, unfiltered and with 20/20 hindsight. I thought back to the very moment she begged me to take her with me at the beginning of my career and could only regrettably shake my head. I had learned yet another invaluable lesson at the expense of a relationship with my daughter. I should have been a man about it, stuck to my guns and established myself first before trying to take her in. Again, I felt emasculated in a sense but this time with less anger and more determination than ever to never put myself is this situation again; even though I had to start over a second time dealing with the same woman. Lesson learned.

The Male Principle: Restoring Manhood

So let's get down to brass tax. Why did I go through this diatribe about my experiences with my first two children and their mothers? The explanations, though complex in detail, are quite simple. 1. To create a foundation from which to teach a lesson. 2. To reveal the error to expose a solution, which would lead a young male to fully, realize, exercise and personify the male principle in his own lives. 3. To foster a deeper understanding of the principles of manhood that will inherently promote making manly decisions, not bad decisions.

Let's face facts. The core concept of manhood and the male principle are under siege on all fronts; through mass media, the criminal justice system, true manhood is on the defense, from the anatomical significance, which defines the word manliness to the psychological modalities of manly behavior through to the spiritual ordinance engendering the male principle. Even the simplest definition of what it means to be a man is being eroded, transfixed, bastardized, and transformed and down-right spat-upon in virtually every way. The evidence is all around us and at every turn and the responsibility of correcting this problem falls squarely in the shoulders of the real true men among us.

You see, the fundamental problem with my situation was not child support or having children prematurely, the problem was in the decision-making process itself, the fundamental understanding of what it means to be a man and the principles, which define it. To share a lesson that I was not taught outside of hearing the stories of how my father married young – out of lust and due to a pregnancy neither he or the woman who conceived his children were ready for and how his son's mother kept them from him and prevented him from becoming a part of their lives. What was missing was connecting the dots, the walk-through, and the play-by-play of the problem through to the solutions. My father was a great and amusing storyteller but the true lesson was sometimes lost in the story. Further still, his two sons, my brothers, never benefited from the insights from his life experiences because he was unable to be present in their lives; much like my children will never be exposed to most of my experiences. In retrospect, I see how the situations with my children mirrored my father's and how generationally, the absent-father motif had manifested itself across generations. In effect, the cycle he created repeated itself in my life. This realization further underscores the fundamental need for men who exemplify manhood to teach men the true principles of manhood. In my opinion, this is the only way to put the *Man* back in the word *manhood*. While the male principle cannot be fully defined in the span of these few pages, my experiences has revealed a few core principles that will spark the conversation and hopefully lend credence to this notion.

The Male Principle Defined

Men Are the Spark. Our world is built on the principle of duality, which manifests as males and females in all living creatures from insects to humans. When these principles coalesce through mating, you have creation. Within that union, the male

136

principle is **the initiator, the starter, the protector, and the spark that leads the way.** You see this in the animal kingdom as a mating dance or ritual of some kind. In humans, males are the ones that initiate courting and provide the spark or seed that initiates the creation of life. Therein lies the responsibility inherent to the male principle and being men. Men are endowed with the responsibility of bearing the seeds of life for humanity. Men initiate the process of bringing souls into this physical dimension and when this process is initiated irresponsibly without the proper mental state and intention - as with my drunken one-night stands - life is created without the benefit of wisdom to shepherd the life that is ultimately brought into this world. My son was created by a union fueled by lust, not by wisdom, which forced his mother to have to embody both the male and female role, which pushed her beyond her natural role as the receiver, the nurturer, the fertile soil that supports the growth of the seed. In my case, a son was brought forward, and I was largely absent and unable to bestow my wisdom to him. Too often today, single women are charged with raising young males, because they are forced to such as in my case. In many instances, this leads to grown males that don't act like men, yet they are endowed with the spark of life. Fundamentally, leads to a range of consequences and behaviors among the children created from such unions. Children by nature emulate parents and gravitate towards the parent of the same sex. When one parent is absent, the child will emulate the behaviors and mannerisms of the parent that is present. Young girls raised by fathers tend to be tomboys whereas young men raised by mothers tend to have feminine mannerisms.

Men Are Leaders. The family is the most basic unit of society and of community. Biblically speaking, within the bounds of marriage between a man and a woman, the man is the head of the family. Even in basic courtships, outside of marriage or biblical constructs, men generally take the lead, set the tone of activity, and regardless of what roles are fulfilled beyond that, the man is considered the head. Growing up, my father was the leader of our family, he established and enforced the house rules and imposed discipline when they weren't followed. This was his natural role as a man. My mother on the other hand, made the house beautiful, comfortable and kept it clean and she was comfortable fulfilling that role. Even in anatomical terms, men have two heads, one for thought and one that initiates the spark of creation. In society, men are largely represented in leadership roles such as politicians, CEOs, church leaders and the like. Fundamental to this is the aspect of the male principle related to leadership and decision-making. As I look back on the circumstances surrounding the birth of my son, I wasn't exercising good sound decision making. My lustful nature and alcohol-impaired judgement produced a child I wasn't ready for and I didn't understand how to be a leader in that situation. Although I eventually found my way, by the grace of God, his mother was strong and raised him to be a responsible young man with minimal help from me. For that, I am eternally thankful as I see examples every day of how his life could have turned out.

Men Live with Conviction and by Action. Perhaps the greatest examples I have witnessed in my lifetime of this aspect of the male principle are in the Civil Rights movement of the 1960s led by Dr. Martin Luther King, Jr. and the Fruit of Islam movement created by The Honorable Elijah Muhammed, later led by Malcolm X and today by Louis Farrakhan. No matter what religion you believe in, these three men personify conviction and exemplify action. Through their uncompromising belief and steadfast actions, they changed the world, as we know it and their examples have inspired me throughout my life. The power of their conviction was and is truly divine. In relating to my own life, I possessed conviction but lacked action. The paralyzing impact of my fear of fatherhood stunted my actions although I was convicted by the desire to be a better father. In the end, my conviction and actions merged, and I arrived on the other side a better man.

Men Have Foresight and Discernment. I haven't mentioned my daughter in this chapter nearly as much as my son. That is simply because I was far younger when my son was born and more experienced in manhood by the time my daughter arrived. I mention her now because my experience with her mother is a perfect example of how not recognizing the gift of foresight that we all have can lead you astray. When I mention foresight, it's not some mystical power, it's simply understanding and recognizing that people are their parents and the residual impact of their upbringing. I'm no exception in this regard. I know early on that my daughter's mother was raised without her father and that her mother had a very strong influence on her. Yet, I ignored these obvious signs of instability, childishness and selfishness out of what I felt at the time was love. In my naivety, I failed to foresee that she idolized her mother to the degree that she wanted to raise a child by herself and joined a church to justify asking me to move out. I recall my father telling me once that if I wanted to see who a woman would be in 20 years, look at her mother. I can only add also look at her upbringing and her relationships with both of her parents. As a man, choosing the right mate is essential to your individual success and the success of your current and future family. My errant choice in women robbed me of a closer relationship with my daughter.

Manhood under Siege

While the experiences I shared in this chapter stem from a degree of irresponsibility, I relate them to the title of *Manhood*

139

under Siege for the simple fact that true manhood is lacking today and is truly under attack. True principles of manhood are not being promoted or taught. On a grand scale, we're witnessing the results of men not being men, and men not teaching younger generations the principles of manhood. While the reasons are vast and varied, at the crux of the attack on manhood today is manhood itself and it has been propagated over generations leading back to slavery. The evidence is all around us and at every turn. While scientists and scholars theorize that this redefinition of masculinity could be deemed a side effect of humanity's evolving consciousness, the spiritually discerning eye would bear witness to a pervasive attack on the male principle that crosses the boundaries of nature into the realm of the perverse. No matter where your spiritual aperture is set, no man of sound mind, regardless of religious, spiritual or sexual persuasion, can deny that in 2019 manhood is under siege. It's time for real men to stand up and put the "MAN" back in Manhood!

~Dedication~

Willie E. Rose (Grandfather, Valdosta, GA - Deceased)

Willie Mack Rose (Father – The Villages, FL)

James Edward Rose (Uncle – Conyers, GA - Deceased)

Alonzo Rose, Sr. (Great-Uncle - Valdosta, GA – Deceased)

Jarell Jefferson-Rose (Son – Beaufort. SC)

Malik Sowell (Stepson – Atlanta, GA)

Biography of Dr. Zebedee Sheppard

Dr. Zebedee Sheppard is an Apostle, Pastor, Conference Speaker, Radio and Television Host, Life Coach, and Church Leadership Advisor. He holds to Doctorates in Theology and Divinity. He is the Founder and CEO of Sheppard Ministries Inc. based in Snow Hill, NC. He is also the Pastor of Victory & Dominion World Outreach Center, one church in two locations, located in the town of Snow Hill, NC and the city of Greensboro, NC. In 1998, he founded the Unity Foundation Community Center in Snow Hill NC. Through his foundation, many community programs have been launched to address numerous inner-city problems and health disparities within the county and communities round about.

Dr. Sheppard travels consistently throughout the country as well as to several nations of the world preaching and teaching the Gospel of Jesus Christ. He also speaks in prisons, schools, and colleges motivating everyone to rise up and live their dream. Dr. Sheppard's heart for missions and the mission field often leads him to numerous foreign missions to assess issues, to instill hope and inspiration to the least among us, and to provide support and resources to those in need. Dr. Sheppard has a passion for mentoring young boys and empowering men to live out their full potential.

Dr. Sheppard is married to the beautiful Dr. Suzanne Evans Sheppard and they have two children Kevan and Keshonna.

Personal Profile

Key Words

Leadership, Passion, Purpose, Perseverance, Faith

Favorite Quote

"Some things won't change until you do." ~ Zebedee Sheppard

Values

Purpose Driven, Empowering Others, Dream Building

Marketable Skills

Vision Coaching, Motivational Speaker, Broadcaster

Contact Information

Email: vdwoc@aol.com

Facebook: Zebedee Sheppard

Twitter: Zebedee Sheppard

THE PORTRAIT OF A MAN

Dr. Zebedee Sheppard

As I consider the topic of this book, "Men Magnifying Manhood," there are many ideologies about manhood we could consider. I remember reading an article about an interview done by rap legend Ice-T for The Guardian back in 2014. In the interview, he was asked about the lyrics on his new album "Manslaughter" from his old thrash metal group Body Count. When asked about the reference "manhood's dead," Ice-T replied, "I think right now you're dealing with the pussyfication of the male sex. Men are just being so passive, not standing for something; they're very politically correct. He stated, "This has nothing to do with the gay male. The gay male is gay, and I have no problem with that. Men are just soft. It's okay to say you want to be a woman but try to be a man and there's something wrong with that." He also stated that, "Women want power. But at the same time, they've made men feel uncomfortable about speaking their feelings."

In this interview, Ice-T expressed a sentiment held widely by men in not only this nation but also even other nations of the

145

world. For quite some time, there's been an effort by various feminist groups in our culture to not only soften, but even kill our manhood. Their objective seems to be to take away the strong masculine qualities that make men who they truly are to the core. We may not like the bluntness of his expression but if we would truly admit it, we would all have to agree that Ice- T has a point. Feminism is dominating every sphere of our society. While I think it is important to call out bad behavior in men, I don't believe that being a strong confidant male who believe in leading and caring for his family is a bad thing. Our world is in desperate need of men who are strong mentally, spiritually, emotionally, and socially. In this hour, we must have men who in their truest form will be models of character, strength and integrity for the next generation. Without a true portrait of a man, it will be very difficult for boys to fully embrace their manhood in a world being plagued by feminism.

What does *Men Magnifying Manhood* really mean? Merriam-Webster defines **manhood** as: **1:** The state or quality of being a man or adult male person; male maturity. **2:** Qualities associated with men: Manliness. **3:** The condition of being an adult male as distinguished from a child or female. To **magnify** means to **1a**: Extol or to praise highly **b:** to cause to be held in greater esteem or respect. **2a:** to increase in significance: Intensify.

This subject has been of great interest to me for over twenty-five years; magnifying manhood and mentoring young boys as well as men to understand their role and purpose in life. I've been pastoring now for 27 years and for the past 22 years I have hosted a yearly conference at my church which I call, "David's Mighty Men Conference." This conference focuses on a model for developing and empowering men taken from 1 Samuel 22 in the Holy Bible. In this chapter, more than 400 men sought out King David who was hiding in a cave at a remote town called Adullam. I call this experience the first official man cave. A man cave as you know is a designated place in a man's home where he can retreat to be alone or to get away from everyone in the house. These men came to the cave of Adullam to retreat with David for his leadership, empowerment, and developmental skills. The Scripture reveals that these men had varying issues they needed help with. 1 Sam.22:1 says, *"And everyone that was in distress, and everyone that was in debt, and everyone that was discontented, gathered themselves unto him; and he became a captain over them: and there were with him about four hundred men."*

Now just think…these men wanted help. They wanted to maximize their manhood and be able to stand tall in their society in that day. These men understood the need for a captain, a coach, and a mentor. They sought out David because he was the perfect role model they could learn from. The story reveals that David became their leader and through a series of events and training, he transformed more than six hundred men into mighty men. They became a militia like no other.

Today more than ever, there is still a need for male leadership models that boys and men can look to as examples as they grow and develop into mature men. Like David, we must magnify manhood. As I fore stated, today manhood as God has designed it is under attack from various entities in our culture whose ultimate plan and desire is to redefine and minimize manhood. Just consider the fact that today our homes, and our communities, and our nation is in shambles because of the lack of father's in the homes.

Every day in the news, we are reminded of the fact that there is a father-crisis in our nation. The lack of father's in the home in my opinion is a national emergency. Recent statistics reveal that in the United States, more than 64 million men identify themselves as

147

being a father. Out of that figure, only 26.5 million men are part of a home where they are married to a spouse and have children under the age of 18 living there. *(Lifeisbeautiful.org)*

According to the U.S. Census Bureau, out of 19.7 million children, more than 1 in 4, live without a father in the home. Research show that when a child is raise in a father- absent home, he or she is affected in the following ways:

1. There is a four times greater risk of poverty.
2. They are more likely to have behavior problems.
3. They are more likely to face abuse and neglect.
4. More likely to abuse drugs and alcohol.
5. More likely to commit a crime.
6. More likely to go to prison.
7. 7 times more likely to become pregnant as a teen.
   (Fatherhood.org)

At the age of twenty-one, I started working at a medium custody male institution that housed over five-hundred inmates. This new career gave me the opportunity to meet men of all ages, all races, and from every background. Men who had not only lost their freedom but so much more because of the life they chose to live. Understanding and realizing my purpose in life gave me the motivation I needed each day as I walked behind those prison walls. I knew my reason for being there was about much more than a receiving a pay check. I knew God had placed me there in that dangerous environment to be a male leadership role model to inspire and encourage men to look beyond their conviction and find redemption. My assignment was to help them realize that failure was not final, and God was there to help each of them find their true identity and purpose in life. Almost every man at some point in his life will struggle with failure. Failure is one of man's greatest fears and it is important for men to know that failure is not final. Failure is only a pause in the process to success. Everyone fails. However, when we fail as men, we do not quit. Success happens when we refuse to quit. Success happens when we get back up from being knocked down. To succeed in life requires perseverance, and as men we must persevere through every failure, every roadblock, and every dark season we experience in life. It has been said that perseverance and failure cannot co-exist. If you make up in your mind that nothing can stop you from achieving your goals, you will succeed and win. My work in criminal justice was rewarding to me because every day I went to work, and those steel doors closed behind me as I walked inside that prison I knew I was there to instill hope and confidence to someone who had lost their way. Jesus said in Matthew 25:36, *"I was in prison and you came unto me."*

Today the United States has the largest prison population in the world. Men are still going to prison every day at an alarming rate. As of 2016, 2.3 million people were incarcerated in the United States, at a rate of 698 people per 100,000. Also note that in 2016, almost 7 million people were under some type of control by the correction industry (incarcerated, on probation or parole, etc. Another recent statistic revealed that black people in this country are imprisoned at more than 5 times the rate of whites; one in 10 black children has a parent behind bars, compared with about one in 60 white kids, according to the Stanford Center on Poverty & Inequality. (*TheMarshallProject.com*)

These disturbing statistics should alarm and motivate us as a nation to rise up and do something to change this narrative and effectively address this growing epidemic. In December 2018, President Donald Trump sign a new bipartisan prison reform bill called, "The First Step Act" which cuts short multiple thousands of prison sentences for federal inmates who have committed low drug offenses making thousands of them immediately available for parole or release.

The Bible says in Proverbs 29:18 (KJV)," *Where there is no vision, the people perish: but he that keepeth the law, happy is he."* The Christian Standard Bible says it this way, *"Without revelation people run wild, but one who follows divine instruction will be happy."* In this scripture, King Solomon is speaking to us about the importance of having a clear path for the future for everyone. Without it, many people will lose hope and will resort to all sorts of unlawful practices to get what they want.

We must provide a pathway of hope for the future for everyone. As a nation, we must not forget the poor and needy or the least among us. We have a duty: lift those in poverty, provide better housing, eradicate hunger, provide better jobs, better wages and benefits, and greater opportunities for low-income families. Life is better when people have value and a sense of worth about themselves.

I believe inside of every boy that there is a leader. However, from a child, that boy must be under the guidance and tutelage of his father or a father figure to fully comprehend his role as a male leader both in the home and in society. I was fortunate enough to have my father at home and in my life until he died at age 68. I also had five brothers who were older than I was. Therefore, there was a lot of masculinity parading through our home when I was a boy that helped me develop into manhood. There are tremendous advantages to children who have active father figures in their lives. Boys learn best about manhood from the men in their lives. This is why a father's presence in the home is so crucial. When there is a father in the home, his authoritative parenting will lead to better emotional, academic, social, and behavioral outcomes for the children overall.

During our annual David's Mighty Men Conference, my objective is to address important topics men are confronted with most in their personal lives. There is a popular Q & A segment in which I allow men to discuss whatever subject they desire. Before the segment begins, the men are asked to write down any question they would like to have addressed during the segment and place it in a box to remain anonymous. During the segment, I along with a team of leaders from various backgrounds will do our best to give an educated answer to the questions pulled from the box. We also take verbal questions as well. What I have discovered is that men get more from this type of setting because they get a chance to hear questions and answers they thought they were the only one struggling with. This session with men proves to be very therapeutic because it provides immediate relief to many men who finally got the chance to get off their chest painful secrets and overwhelming guilt they've been carrying for many years. During this session, many men even feel comfortable enough to confess their most intimate struggles. What they discover is that many of the issues they have been struggling with in the dark are only common to man.

Manhood is about conquering private struggles. Private struggles are just that, things we struggle with in private. Things that the Apostle Paul said in Hebrews 12:1, we allow to get us off course so easily. In this chapter, Paul admonishes us to lay aside every weight and sin that easily trips us up, so we can run with patience and win the race set before us.

Let's view Hebrews 12:1 in The New Living Translation. *"Therefore, since we are surrounded by such a huge crowd of witnesses to the life of faith, let us strip off every weight that slows us down, especially the sin that so easily trips us up. And let us run with endurance the race God has set before us."*

The writer of Hebrews points out the fact that we all struggle with something, but as we mature into manhood we should do as an Olympic runner does in a race. We should strip off the excess weight and vices so we can run and win the race set before us. I believe maximizing our manhood requires living a life of discipline. Which reminds me of another key verse by Apostle Paul found in 1 Corinthians 13:11 that says, *"When I was a child, I spoke as a child, I understood as a child, I thought as a child; but when I became a man, I put away childish things."* As we grow from childhood into adulthood there should be a noticeable difference in the way we live, the way we handle problems, and in the way we carry ourselves. Manhood is marked by maturity, honor, integrity, strength, seriousness, responsibility etc. It is about facing life's challenges head on with confidence. When I talk about private struggles, I'm talking about the inner proclivities that can ruin our lives and our testimonies if left unchecked.

Here are some facts about private struggles I shared during one of my conferences:

1. Everybody has them. Don't ever think you're alone in your struggle. This is where Satan messes with your mind. He wants you to think you are all alone in your struggle. You would be surprised at the number of people you know who are going through the same struggle you are facing.

2. Even those we admire most and consider our role models have private struggles.

3. No one wants their private struggle to become public, especially if they haven't overcome it.

4. Some struggles are more difficult to overcome if they are kept private. You've heard the old saying, "confession is good for the soul." There's a lot of truth to that statement because some struggles must be shared with someone who

can assist you and help you overcome it. Not to mention getting it out in the open take a load of pressure off our chest and our conscious.

5. Never forget the fact that there is no struggle you cannot overcome by the power and grace of God.

In 2 Corinthians 12:9 (NKJV) God said, *"My grace is sufficient for you, for My strength is made perfect in weakness."* This verse is saying God has enough grace to make you an overcomer in every struggle you face no matter the severity or however long it takes. What private issues are you struggling with that you want to desperately overcome? You have obviously prayed about it numerous times, so what other steps can you take to overcome your struggle. Let me suggest seven things that has helped many men overcome their struggles:

1. First, humble yourself before God and confess the struggle to him.

2. Ask him to give you the grace to overcome your struggle once and for all.

3. If someone else at some point has victimized you in your life, as difficult as it may be, forgive the perpetrator. Your forgiveness doesn't free the perpetrator as much as it frees you.

4. Be fully determined to do whatever is necessary to overcome your struggle.

5. Find someone like a specialist or a support group you can trust, that has a track record for helping people overcome what you are struggling with and commit yourself to them.

6. Whatever the commitment requires, stick it out, until you've conquered the struggle.

7. Once you are free or have control of the struggle, live a life of discipline so it can never entangle you again.

~Dedication~

Kevan M. Sheppard. – Kinston, NC

Kemori I. Sheppard. – Kinston, NC

Jalen Jones – Kinston, NC

Justin Ashford – Goldsboro, NC

Tyrone Dudley Jr – Snow Hill, NC

Tevin Pittman – Kinston, NC

Syquan Williams – Snow Hill, NC

Noah Mason – Greenville, NC

Jay P. Morgan – Ayden, NC

Javier Scott - Greenville

156

Biography of Dr. Kristofer C. Smith

Dr. Kristofer C. Smith was born and raised in Metro Atlanta, Georgia. Dr. Kristofer C. Smith is a 2009 graduate of Florida Agricultural and Mechanical University with a Doctor of Pharmacy degree.

Dr. Smith is currently a Specialty Pharmacist with Encompass Rx Specialty Pharmacy, specializing in the pharmacological management of patients with specific diseases for which specialized medication therapy is required.

Dr. Smith loves God and loves people. He actively serves in the church as a trustee board member at both Higher Calling Ministries in Decatur, Georgia and Freedom Fellowship Church in Atlanta, Georgia; and as a Sunday School Teacher at Higher Calling Ministries.

Dr. Smith is also an active volunteer with a number of non-profit organizations including Beulah Urban Outreach, The Extraordinary League, and The Orchid Project.

Each day, Dr. Smith strives to learn something new, implement something he has learned, and pass on something he has learned to encourage someone else. His goal is to live each day of his life with intent.

Personal Profile

Key Words

Love, Relationship, Faith, Purpose

Favorite Quote

"I can't do equals I won't do." ~ Dr. Kristofer C. Smith

Values

Honesty, Integrity, Character, Family

Marketable Skills

Public Speaking, Medication Counseling, Health Fairs

Contact Information

Email: kcsmith03@hotmail.com

Website: www.theextraordinaryleague.com

LinkedIn.com: Kristofer Smith, PharmD, MSCS

MANHOOD: STRENGTH TO LOVE

Dr. Kristofer C. Smith

One of my favorite things to do, as a growing boy in a two-parent household, was to watch television. If it were up to me, I would watch television every single day and at any time of the day. I remember rising early Saturday mornings to watch Looney Toons, and staying up late summer nights to watch reruns of Sanford and Son, Good Times, and 227. I even recall rising as early as 5am most weekday mornings, of my high school years, to catch the morning news.

While I enjoyed watching as much television as possible, I also recall the restrictions my parents placed on my younger brother and me as children. In my opinion, the ferocity with which they (especially my father) enforced these restrictions. For example, we were only allowed to watch television for an hour a day on school nights and all homework must have been completed before the television could be watched. Shows like wrestling and Power Rangers were deemed too violent. Rated "R" movies cursed too much. TV series' such as Fresh Prince, Living Color,

159

Martin, and The Simpsons, were deemed too mature for our eyes and ears. My father even tried to restrict me from bringing my television with me to college.

Unfortunately, for me, such restrictions on television were only a microcosm of greater rules and restrictions enforced in my father's household. Other restrictions usually included no parties and dances, no listening to such genres of music as rap and rhythm and blues, no staying out past 10PM on non-school nights, no sleeping past 10AM during the summer months, and no disrespecting my elders.

Lest I forget all the household chores that had to be completed. Having to find my own way to school, as I grew older, having to find rides home from baseball practice or band practice, and even having to pay rent during the summer months I came home from college.

During these formative years of my life, I had a problem with such rules and restrictions. I felt that they were too restrictive, and that this tyrannical, dictator-like, ruler of my life was unreasonable and unnecessary. I was mostly a well-mannered and well-behaved young man, yet when it pertained to rules and restrictions, I was sometimes sneaky and dishonest, and usually disobedient. I know that is hard to believe for those that know me, except for my younger brother. I usually snuck and watched the television; although my father usually knew I was watching anyway. I usually waited until 5AM of the next school day to start and complete homework due that day, sometimes completing the homework right before class. I sometimes went to bed without completing my required chores only to be awakened to a shouting mother or a belt-yielding father to complete the chores.

Such disobedience usually caused much tension between my father and me as I often butted heads with him on those rules and even asked, "What are you trying to do to me?" The result was usually the thought that "I don't want to be like my father when I grow up. I will not raise my children like this."

Fast forward to the present, as a 34-year-old, African American male with a doctorate degree, serving others as a registered pharmacist, volunteer, and church leader. I am behind on many television shows and movies; I am pretty anal about cleanliness, and I am usually awake most mornings before the sun rises.

I find that I am becoming more like my father with each passing day, and instead of being ashamed of this reality, I am actually grateful and honored to be compared to him. As I stated at his funeral in 2017, I would not be the man that many know me to be, if not for the great man that raised me.

1 Corinthians 13:11 (KJV) states, *"When I was a child, I spake as a child, I understood as a child, I thought as a child: but when I became a man, I put away childish things."* As I have grown into manhood, my perspective of my childhood has changed dramatically. No longer do I think of my childhood with disdain for the rules and restrictions that were put in place, nor do I think of my father as a dictator who ruled with an iron fist as a means to control. Instead, I am thankful for my sheltered childhood that has kept me grounded in a vast world full of possibilities and beauty, but yet also extremely dangerous. I now understand that the rules and restrictions were not meant to be tools to control me, but were put in place because my parents, more specifically my father considering the title of the book, loved me and were teaching me to be a man.

Defining manhood in today's society can be downright confusing. On one hand, you're a man if you rule with an iron fist, are physically built like a linebacker, or you have a good job making good money. On the other hand, you're a man if you're in touch with your feelings, or you embrace your emotional being. Yet, there are some who define manhood by sexual prowess. However, might I suggest, that true manhood is defined not by these things but is defined how a man loves.

Matthew 22:37-40 (KJV) states, *"Jesus said unto him, Thou shalt love the Lord thy God with all thy heart, and with all thy soul, and with all thy mind. This is the first and great commandment. And the second is like unto it, Thou shalt love thy neighbor as thyself. On these two commandments hang all the law and prophets."*

Love is a word that is often misunderstood, and often associated with strong emotions. Love is all encompassing, and hard to fully explain, because in my opinion, to know love is to know God, and according to 1 John 4:8 (KJV), *"God is love."* The purpose of this chapter is not to define what love is, but to magnify manhood through the lens of love. Therefore, it is important to define what love is. Subsequently, I present to you a simple, yet profound, definition of love, defined by a good friend of mine who states, "Love is when you look in the mirror, and no longer see yourself." (G. Spencer) This is a profound definition of love because through this statement we can conclude that love is selfless, love is sacrificial, and love is about serving others. As we magnify manhood through the lens of love, we will see that the basis of manhood is built on the foundation of humility, selflessness, sacrifice, self-control and leadership; all attributes which point to love, which points to God.

At the beginning of this chapter, I presented to you a father (and mother) who raised me and my siblings in an environment of rules and restrictions that I initially perceived to be at times unreasonable, but that I now understand to be necessary because of the love he (and she) had for us. However, it would not be prudent of me if I did not share the numerous examples of love he (and she) showed us also throughout these formative years; love that far outweighed the perceived thoughts of control.

My siblings and I grew up as children of a pastor. If I could describe him from my perspective, I would describe him as a giant of a man with a thunderous voice that could strike fear in you if you were doing something wrong. However, most of the time he was a gentle giant; a humble man; a man of integrity and good character; an honest man with a heart of gold, that loved his wife, his family, his church, his friends, his enemies, and most importantly, God. My father's love for God, and his humble submission to the will of God, laid a foundation for a household full of love, and an example of manhood that would be difficult to match or surpass.

Keeping in mind our definition of love, my father could be described as a selfless and sacrificial man. He was often the last person to go to bed at night and many times, the first person to awake in the mornings. Before I was old enough to go back and forth myself, he would take me to school most mornings and he would pick me up most days.

He was the main cook of the household, as my mother would cook primarily on the weekends. I remember eating together most nights as a family, and many of those nights, chicken was on the menu. My favorite parts of the chicken were the leg and the thigh, while my parents always ate the breast and the wing. However, one day I recall my father eating a thigh instead of a breast, and asked him why he didn't eat the breast as I thought the breast was his favorite. His response was that he actually preferred the leg and the thigh, but only ate the breast because he knew I also preferred the leg and thigh. Who knew all those years he sacrificed eating his favorite parts of the chicken so that I could enjoy them. Wow! Just one small example of the many selfless, sacrificial acts of love he displayed to me as his son.

My father was also a provider. I never had to worry about where my next meal was coming from, whether I had clothes on my back or shoes on my feet, or a roof over my head. My father provided all of these things and more because he knew, I was dependent on him to supply my needs. I believe a man as a provider presents an image for how God desires us to trust Him. As our heavenly father, God knows what we need before we ask, and will supply what we need because we are His children and He loves us. So, when we are uncertain about needs being met, God does not want us to worry. Instead, He wants us to confidently trust Him, just at a child trusts his or her parents to provide for the needs that they have, without worry.

Manhood is not easy. None of us is perfect. In life, we experience disappointments, we experience failures, we fall into temptation, we get angry, and we make many mistakes. However, a true sign of manhood is having the ability to maintain a level of self-control, despite the numerous imperfections of this world. My father was not a perfect man. There were times he would be pushed to anger, times he made mistakes, and I'm sure times he was tempted. However imperfect he was, I am grateful that he exhibited enough self-control that he never abused his wife or his children. He always treated us with respect, and he sought forgiveness for any wrongs he may have done. He cherished the gift from God who is my mother and loved her as Christ loved the church, and he brought his children up in the nurture and admonition of the Lord.

A true leader was my father. He understood the importance of having a relationship with God. Through his relationship with

God, he gained the tools necessary to courageously lead his wife, family, and congregation. He led by example. He led by serving. He taught us that we were accountable to God for our own lives and the decisions we made.

I am reminded of a specific Father's Day in which all of these attributes of manhood were on full display. I was attending Florida A & M University during the summer semester, and the plan was to meet my parents' home in Atlanta, Georgia that Father's Day afternoon to celebrate my father on this special day. First, my parents had to travel to Alabama for a preaching engagement my father was to fulfill. I left Tallahassee, Florida early Sunday morning for Atlanta with one service light on in my car. By the time, I reached the halfway point of my trip and was on the freeway to Atlanta, all my services lights were lit in my car, and by the time, I pulled into a store lot just off the freeway, my car completely shut down.

I tried to take care of it myself, as I knew to do. I got a jump from a man who fully charged my battery, and was back on the move toward the freeway. However, my car shut down again just after I made it back to the same store lot where my car originally shut down. With no other options at this point, and in an unfamiliar place, I called my parents who said they would come after my father finished his preaching engagement.

After a few hours, my parents arrived from Alabama. My father jumpstarted my car and we were on the road to Atlanta. Unfortunately, the car stopped two more times on our road to Atlanta, after which my mother and I became frustrated. By this time, we had replaced the battery and the alternator, and it was now dark outside. We were just outside of Atlanta and I wanted to leave the car where it was, but my father had not given up. He decided to jumpstart the car again and drive it himself while we followed behind. He pulled off before we did and by the time we caught up to him, the car had stopped again and he was literally pushing the car at the age of 69 or 70 years old.

We decided to leave the car there and have it towed in the morning and went home. When we arrived home, I apologized to my father because Father's Day had not gone according to plan. I'll never forget his response to me in that moment as he said, "This is what being a father is all about." In that experience alone, I watched my father take the lead in a crisis, sacrificially give up his day to make provision for me. Selflessly take on the burden of getting us home and humbly understand that a father's responsibility never takes a break, even on father's day; all while maintaining the self-control to stay calm in the midst of crisis, and keep us calm during what was a most frustrating experience.

Now I am not naive to the fact that many reading this chapter may not share a similar experience of fatherhood and manhood as I have. I understand many were raised in a fatherless home for many reasons. Many may have been raised with a single father, an inconsistent father, a stepfather, a male figure other than a father, or no male figure at all.

No matter what your past is, I challenge each man reading this chapter to embrace manhood by having the strength to love. What has happened in your past is in your past. It cannot be changed, so do not give it power over your present. God has given each of us free will to choose, so choose to love your wives, families, friends, and enemies with humility, selflessness, sacrifice, self-control, and leadership.

Look no further than the example of Jesus Christ when trying to find out how to embrace manhood through love. Jesus led those who believed from sin toward a righteous relationship with God. He submitted to the will of the Father, by selflessly sacrificing His life, so that His shed blood would cleanse us of all our sins, providing us a path toward reconciliation with God. The ultimate act of manhood, done simply because He chose to love us unconditionally.

~Dedication~

Victor P. Smith (In Memoriam)

Arthur L. Johnson (In Memoriam)

Jerry Smith (In Memoriam)

Napoleon Johnson, Sr (In Memoriam)

Paul Smith, Snellville, GA

Eric Smith, Decatur, GA

Terrence Burney, Decatur, GA

Floyd Thomas, Decatur, GA

Joseph C. Smith, Jr, Decatur, GA

Arthur D. Johnson, Detroit, MI

Freddie Purry, Detroit, MI

Marshaun Green, San Marcos, TX

Victor Smith, Snellville, GA

Tyler Smith, Snellville, GA

Patrick Smith, Snellville, GA

Miles Green, San Marcos, TX

Biography of Derrick Taylor

Derrick Taylor is a very new school speaker with an old school flavor. Born in Los Angeles, California but raised in Kinston NC, he graduated from Kinston High School. He began ministry at Jumping Run Church in LaGrange, NC, under the leadership of Pastor W. Anthony Lawson II, by assisting with Youth Ministry while in his teen years and acknowledging his call to ministry. After graduation, he earned culinary training then moved to Durham NC. He began attending Mount Zion Christian Church under the leadership of Apostle Donald Q. Fozard, Sr. While at Mount Zion, he continued his call to preach and began attending Hosanna Bible College. He preached his initial sermon at Mt. Zion as well as graduated with a Bachelors in Theology and Masters of Divinity from the college.

He currently serves at Mt. Zion Church in various capacities, including Mass Choir, Minister, and Follow-Up Committee. He is the father of two loving daughters, Abriana Simone and Jada Dominique. He maintains "A Standard to Keep and A God to Glorify!"

Personal Profile

Key Words

Purpose, Vision, Dedication, Love

Favorite Quote

"When God Gets Ready to Raise You Up, Can't No Devil in Hell Keep You Down!" ~ Derrick Taylor

Values

Visionary, Chain Breaker, Forward Thinker

Marketable Skills

Leadership, Entrepreneurship

Contact Information

Email: Ministerderrick@gmail.com

Facebook: www.facebook.com/ministerderricktaylor

NO LONGER THE PRISONER

Derrick Taylor

I was 24 years old in 2002 when an exceptional movie was released entitled *Antwone Fisher.*[3] This movie has sense become one of my favorite movies. The film highlights the life of the temperamental Antwone Fisher who entered the U.S. Navy and the unfolding of his upbringing. While I've never aspired to join the military, there were some similarities to Antwone's life that brought me to attention. As this story unfolds, the objective is to bring you to the realization that you can get out of any prison you are in; whenever you want to. You do not have to live as a prisoner forever. You can be free and declare that you are *No Longer the Prisoner*!

"Train up a child in the way he should go: and when he is old, he will not depart from it."[4]

---

[3] Washington, Denzel, director. Antwone Fisher. IMDb, IMDb.com, 10 Jan. 2003.

[4] Proverbs 22: 6. Outskirts Press, 2012.

My family was quite religious so consequently I grew up in church. Ever since I can remember, all I've known is church. Being born in 1978 in Los Angeles, California, I remember our first house being directly across the street from our church. I often believed we lived at the church and just slept across the street at the house. We went to church so much, we knew who was going to dance, run, yell, and all stops in between. Being the only child at the time, myself and my cousins who I've grown to call brothers and sister, would "play church" at home. If I remember correctly, Bobby was the Pastor, I was the choir, Pam was the Evangelist, Ray and everybody else was whatever we told them to be!

Physical Prison

"When Nothing Else Could Help, Love Lifted Me!"[5]

In 1985, I moved to North Carolina with my aunt and uncle who were stationed at Camp Lejeune Marine Base in Jacksonville, N.C. I wasn't completely sure why the quick move and away from my birth parents, but I'd grow to understand it later. From this point forward, it became a back and forth residential situation between the new family setup as opposed to what we had considered a normal upbringing with Mom and Dad. This was my new normal. As the years passed by, our family remained faithful to regular church attendance. Thank God we weren't going as much as we did in Los Angeles, but we were there every time the doors opened nonetheless. I became much closer to my new family dynamic as opposed to living with my own mother. I actually began to hate living with her. I think one of the first bouts of hatred

---

[5] Rowe, James. *Love Lifted Me*. 1911.

came from being in the fifth grade and running up the telephone bill; calling 1-900 numbers. I'll spare you the details of the whipping I received, but it made me call 911 on her for beating me with a frying pan. Humorous as it may sound now, this was my beginning of sorrows.

I began acting out. I've always loved education but in the latter years of elementary school, I was responsible for getting up and catching the bus to school. I would wake up around 10AM and have to run to school. I would get there just in time for lunch. This behavior went on for a short time until the principal and teachers caught wind of my pattern and had a parent-teacher conference. My erratic behaviors escalated which prompted her to put me in a group home. Here I am in the fifth grade, in an environment with these teenage kids. The difference with me was they were mandated here from the courts, but I was dropped off by the police at the request of my mother. Oh my Lord; I hated her so much at that point! However, this would not be the only time I'd get placed in a detention type facility. I went from the group home to later being placed in a detention center, then off to Dobbs Youth Detention Center in Kinston, N.C. The last time I'd experience incarceration was in my junior year of high school in Arkansas for doing something so stupid I'll spare you the details of explaining. And, we were still going to church.

Why did I go through this? Was I really a bad child? Why did I have to undergo psychiatric evaluations in elementary school? Why did the therapist in Jacksonville, N.C. prescribe me Ritalin? ...Which I never took. Did I have ADHD? Why in the seventh grade did I have to attend classes in the "special kids" program? Maybe I was crazy. I wasn't crazy or special - I felt unloved. More often than not, I hear people saying, "Boys don't show emotion. Don't cry; that's punky, etc." Parents would tell you "do as I say and not as I do; you're a child, so stay in a child's place; your opinion only matters when you get your own place!" In my new family, I felt loved. True, my cousins were not my biological brothers and sisters, but I felt like they wanted me around. From the parental equation, I felt nothing and felt like nothing.

Mental Prison

"Thou wilt keep him in perfect peace, whose mind is stayed on thee: because he trusted in thee."[6]

I believe there is no far more impenetrable prison to be locked up in than that of the mind. When a person's mind is locked up, it shuts down everything. I became locked up physically because I was locked up mentally; and here's why. A good overview I've already mentioned is concerning the physical, but what happened? What happened to me that caused me to just "change" into the bad kid? Let's talk about it.

While I thoroughly enjoyed my new family, I still oftentimes felt unloved. I had the basic necessities but still never felt the love that my cousins received. I felt like I was the fifth wheel; a "spare tire" child. I was good enough to tell jokes and be a walking comedy show, but not good enough to get a hug. I was good enough to take out the trash and clean my room, but never good enough for you to tell me, "I love you!" I was good enough to lock the doors and kill the spiders, but not good enough for you to protect me from the *Big Bad Wolf.*

Who was the *Big Bad Wolf?* Remembering back to the film,

---

[6] Isaiah 26:3. Outskirts Press, 2012.

Antwone's Big Bad Wolf was his older sister who repeatedly molested him and made him feel worthless. My Big Bad Wolf was one of mom's boyfriends who did the same thing to me. My fifth grade school year was the beginning of sorrows for me because it was the first time I'd have a "Big Bad Wolf" experience. My mother would return home from work and notice her clothes and shoes were out of their original place and not knowing I was made to play dress up with her outfits. I was truly in a mental prison. I don't quite remember why they broke up, but it took me years to finally disclose what happened when she was gone. I remember him drinking MD 20/20 and Olde English 800, a 40 0z malt liquor and it took me years to see those bottles and not feel nasty. Growing up, I wanted to die. I hated my life so much that I'd even contemplated so many times ending it. Would I hang myself? No, maybe I'll slit my wrist. Wait, I don't like bleeding so I'll just drink poison. Maybe not because I like drinking Kool-Aid too much. All of those thoughts plagued my mind. I could never come up with a quick, painless solution of how to kill myself. Well, doggone it; I guess I'll just keep living.

I lived with my secret for years. I made friends and even got married and never told anyone what happened. We grew up in church; surely, I couldn't tell anyone that throughout my adolescent, teens, and 20's, I'd experienced that type of trauma. I was a boy and boys don't cry, remember? Boys don't show emotions. I'd always just wanted to be loved. If I told what happened and what I was feeling, no one would believe me. I can't tell my wife because she'd leave. Surely, she didn't marry a man to find out this was in his past. What would the church people think? I was an adult and was still going to church; what do I do? And sure as life would have it, once the cat was out of the bag, life took a tailspin. Here I would find myself divorced, alone, ended and borderline-ended friendships, and back depressed again. I even started going to a counselor to discuss my issues just as Antwone did. I came to a place just as Antwone explained after three sessions with his counselor, actor Denzel Washington, "I don't know what to do." But, I was still going to church…

"Who will cry for the little boy?[7]
Lost and all alone.
Who will cry for the little boy?
Abandoned without his own?

Who will cry for the little boy?
He cried himself to sleep.
Who will cry for the little boy?
He never had for keeps.

Who will cry for the little boy?
He walked the burning sand
Who will cry for the little boy?
The boy inside the man.

Who will cry for the little boy?
Who knows well hurt and pain
Who will cry for the little boy?
He died again and again.

Who will cry for the little boy?
A good boy he tried to be
Who will cry for the little boy?
Who cries inside of me."

---

[7] Fisher, Antwone. Who Will Cry For The Little Boy. 1st ed., William Morrow, 2002.

Jesus Christ, My New Best Friend

"And ye shall know the truth and the truth shall make you free."[8]

I remember when I first began disclosing my story, I wished I had grown up a crack baby, weed head, or something more socially acceptable. Even though we were in church, I could never tell the truth about my upbringing. Grant it, it wasn't all bad. I had some great days with my new family. It wasn't until things got really bad that I had a life changing conversation with two of my spiritual sisters. It wasn't until then that they made me realize what I interpreted as my prison, was not my fault. Wait a minute! You mean to tell me that all these feelings and all these ungodly desires are not my fault? You've got to be kidding me. I did have to take ownership of my own actions at this point being an adult, but the initial hurts and pains of life were not generated by things I did. It wasn't until then that I began putting my life into the right perspective. All of the church attendance started making sense.

"When my father and my mother forsake me, then the Lord will take me up."[9]

I had spent my entire life hiding in the shadows, but it wasn't until I revealed the truth to my aggressive/contrary/confusing life, that life took on another perspective. I had been *going* to church, but I'd never experienced God. He was there the whole time. I had to stop crying because nobody wanted to be my friend. He was my friend the entire time. I had to stop begging for attention and putting on free comedy shows. I didn't have to beg for attention; I

[8] Romans 8:32. Outskirts Press, 2012.
[9] Psalm 27:10. Outskirts Press, 2012.

already had His. I thought I was ugly and stupid. It wasn't until the junior year of my most recent Master's degree at Hosanna Bible College that I actually began believing I was really smart. I knew I had a smart mouth, but not really *smart* smart. I can now look in the mirror and be happy with who I see looking back. I stopped giving wrong people access to my life for the sake of numbers. I realized if and when He's all you've got, He is everything that you need. Once I saw my personal life differently, I saw my new family differently as well. I really think my aunt did the best she could with me, even while dealing with her own children. I really thank God for what I considered my new family because no matter where I found myself in life, they were there. Every graduation, my wedding, initial sermon, and every step in between. It's a shame that here I am now forty years old and I'm just now starting to believe when I hear the words, "I love you," someone actually means it.

What's the Point

"If we confess our sins, he is faithful and just to forgive us our sins and to cleanse us from all unrighteousness."[10]

I fully understand that every man's story is different. My story could read as total left field compared to the things you've gone through. I used *Antwone Fisher* as a canvas to paint my picture. You may have a more *Boyz in the Hood*[11] or *Menace to Society*[12]

[10] 1 John 1:9. Outskirts Press, 2012.

[11] Singleton, John, director. Boyz N the Hood. IMDb, IMDb.com, 12 July 1991.

[12] Hughes, Albert and Allen Hughes, directors. Menace II Society. IMDb, IMDb.com, 26 May 1993.

background, but we all have a background. The thing I've learned is no matter where I was in life, God was there. Grant it, this is a very abbreviated version of my story, but God was there. I saw Him moving in my life when I didn't even want to be alive. I found favor with the people in the youth detention centers; to the point that I have even gone to minister at the same youth centers I was locked up in as a child. When I didn't want to live, I could hear in my spirit, "You can't die now! Something else is around the corner!" Even though my prison may not have been yours, mental prison is still mental prison and physical prison is still a physical prison.

I could have easily taken the approach to impress you with Scriptures and spiritual sayings to wow you, but I'm finding that very unprofitable. Sometimes we as men just want to be loved. I had no idea what love was. I'm just now starting to believe that love actually can exist for me. The reason why is because God's love existed for me even when I was quite the unlovable fella. I want you to understand that pain is a prison too. Feeling unloved is a prison. Being rejected and cast aside is a prison. You do not have to live your life a prisoner. Yes, I was in church too. I knew all the scriptures, took notes, sang, preached, and even prophesied but was still a prisoner. However, I found God to be faithful to me. His word said He would never leave or forsake me and I took that to the bank. He preserved me. He didn't allow me to die when I contemplated suicide multiple times. He kept my mind when my friends and spouse walked away. I was at my lowest and He was still there. I didn't have to beg for His love; it was automatic.

When do you want to get out of prison? Whatever vice the enemy is using to keep you locked up, you can be free. Jesus is faithful to forgive and cleanse you. I do not care what you've done. You can be free. You can live your life prison free. If you will repent of your sins and ask God to be your Father and Jesus your

179

Savior, He will do just that. You don't have to be ashamed of Him because He is definitely not ashamed of you. There is so much that God has in store for your life. I decree and declare that your prison days are over. I prophesy that no weapon the enemy has formed against you will prosper. You are not what your mother, father, school teacher, or anyone else who has spoken evil over you are. You are the head and not the tail. I break the back of every lie and curse it at the root. You will not drive your car off the road or shoot yourself. No matter what you've done, God still loves you. The life you've been dreaming about, it is still attainable. Begin to live out the dreams God has placed in your spirit; that vision of a healthier you, a happier you, a whole you, and a healed you. Every voice that has uttered negativity in your ear or in your direction is a lie. Give attention to the Word of the Lord over your life. Take heed to wisdom and live. Live knowing God is your strength and your provider. You are not a failure; you're more than a conqueror. Never ever return to prison again. I decree and declare that you are *No Longer The Prisoner* you used to be. You are the man God has called for such a time as this. Live in the victory!

~Dedication~

I dedicate this chapter to the following men who have been quite influential in my life and I'm totally honored to call you my brothers, mentors, and mentees; and to the father I know by name but never had the pleasure of growing up with - *Larry R. Ingram*.

Apostle Donald Q. Fozard, Sr

John Bryson

L.B. Taylor, Sr

Bobby Williams

Jonathan Gage

Christopher Hatchell

Ivan Hamm

Carlos Rand

Anthony Brandon Sr

W. Anthony Lawson Sr

Michael Harris

Garland Jones

Bryan Cumberlander

Ronald Rice, Jr

Gerard Green

Donald Fozard, Jr

Titus Fozard

Barney Kennedy

Terry Bristow

Caleb Clark

Anthony Brandon, Jr

Tyler Evans

Lafayette Stern

Donald Stern

Nakiel Williams

Matthew Jackson

Carlton Williams

David Lawrence

Roman Lawrence

Biography of Emmanuel A. Thomas

Emmanuel A. Thomas is a motivational speaker, fashion consultant, and founder of "Courting God's Way." Courting God's Way is a blog that reaches people around the world who are seeking to learn more about relationships, purity, and value. Emmanuel grew up in church and knew of the Gospel, but made his own decision to accept Jesus Christ as his personal Lord and Savior at age twelve. At the age of thirteen, Emmanuel knew that he was called into the ministry to preach the Gospel.

Emmanuel hosted "Talk Show with Emmanuel Thomas" from 2011 until 2015. The show aired weekly as he ministered the Gospel to people around the world. On the show, he also interviewed people of various positions such as pastors, teachers, singers, rappers, actors, and more. Over four thousand people were impacted by Talk Show with Emmanuel Thomas. In 2015, Emmanuel was led to end the show to open his availability to do more outreach and speaking engagements. He is currently taking the Gospel around the world through preaching, teaching, and motivational speaking. Emmanuel is most passionate about helping others discover their purpose, fulfill their dreams, and remain hopeful in the midst of brokenness. Emmanuel currently serves at his church home in Atlanta, Georgia. In his free time, he enjoys reading, writing, traveling, and exploring new adventures with family and friends.

Personal Profile

Key Words

Commitment, Purpose, Relationships, Vision, Value

Favorite Quote

"You had a purpose before anyone had an opinion." ~ Emmanuel A. Thomas

Values

Fulfilling Dreams, Staying Hopeful, Sharing Inspiration, Understanding Vision, Maintaining Healthy Relationships

Marketable Skills

Speaking, Teaching, Fashion Consulting, Mentorship, Social Networking

Contact Information

Email: bookemmanuelthomas@gmail.com

Facebook.com: Emmanuel A. Thomas

Twitter.com: EmmanuelThomas

Instagram: (@iamemmanuelthomas)

PURSUING YOUR PURPOSE WHILE COURTING GOD'S WAY

Emmanuel A. Thomas

I am the prime example of pursuing purpose while courting God's way. I have been courting my beautiful girlfriend for the past six years. We are excited and looking forward to marriage at this point. I was fourteen when I met Angel and she was twelve. We were both young and knew nothing about relationships nor our purpose. I preached from time to time in the youth ministry where we attended and she sang but we were not fully confident in knowing our identity in Christ. I remember the first time I laid eyes on her, I could see a beautiful girl yet someone who was broken. What attracted her to me the most is the fact that we could relate. Growing up, I was always told that I was handsome and dressed well by family members. However, I had low self-esteem because I could not relate to my generation. In elementary school, I was required to wear school uniforms, which included a white or blue polo shirt, black or navy dress pants, and black or brown dress shoes. Since I had to dress like that for school, having that sort of style stuck with me. Even though I did

185

not have to wear a uniform during my middle and high school years, I would continue to dress up for school because that is what I was used to wearing. At that point, dressing up was not a requirement, but a choice.

I always felt comfortable around family; however, I was never comfortable around people at school. My classmates would laugh at me for bringing my Bible to school and reading it during lunchtime. They laughed at me for dressing up and not wearing the new popular shoes or jeans. What made it even worse was the fact that I was overweight during my middle school years. I was weighing about one hundred and eighty pounds in the sixth grade. I can remember girls would tell me, "You are cute and you have good hair, but I would not be able to date you because you dress like a preacher" or "You are handsome but I need a thug, someone who can fight and protect." Hearing this from girls always caused me to believe that I would never have a serious relationship or be married to someone who was truly in love with the guy that God created me to be. I always thought that I was too preppy and churchy. However, in 2010, God brought *my Angel* across my path. I can remember seeing that brokenness and it caused me to want to build a friendship because I was on the same boat. When Angel and I first began talking, she would express how she felt ugly and that no one was truly interested in her natural beauty. I could not believe that she felt that way because she was the most naturally beautiful girl that I had ever seen in my opinion. I can remember praying to God for a girlfriend/wife who loved Christ more than she loved me. I wanted someone who was younger than I was, but still mature. I wanted someone who was petite, in good shape (to help me stay in shape, funny right? – remind you, I was chunky at that time), had brown eyes, and could sing. Surprisingly, Angel had all of those features. She is about two years younger than I am, beautifully petite and in shape. She has those pretty brown eyes, and she can sing her heart out.

God's signs are evident. They are not very hard to understand at all. Oftentimes, as humans we make it hard to understand where God is leading us. However, I knew very clearly that Angel was the one for me. She accepted me for who I was. She liked the fact that I enjoyed dressing up. She loved the fact that I was called into the ministry to preach the Gospel around the world. She thought that my body size was perfect. I thought that she was lying to me. That was the enemy trying to deceive me into thinking that "this girl is just telling you this", "she just wants something from you", "you will never find the perfect girl, remember?". Coming to find out, about a year after we started dating, Angel found a list that she made that listed all of the features that she wanted in a boyfriend/husband. Surprisingly, on her list she had good hair, light skin, tall, loves God, funny, and preppy style. When she looked back at that list, she quickly realized that I had every single feature on her list. The enemy used people to tell us "that does not happen for real", "that's just puppy love", "who would write a list like that", "God can give you better than what is on your list" – Crazy, right? Moreover, what was most disappointing to us was the people who would tell us these things were church people, people who knew the Word – at least we thought they did. At that point, we were around ages sixteen and fourteen. At those tender ages, we were confident that God had created us for each other and wanted eventually to pursue marriage.

I grew up thinking that dating was a distraction. I was taught that if you date someone, you are in a bad place because you are going to be held back from moving forward. However, when I got serious about being in a relationship with Angel, I was more focused on the plans that God had for my life than I had ever been before. One of the reasons why I felt more focused is because

187

Angel always pushed me and continues to push me to move forward and to grow spiritually. I even became healthier. I lost about thirty pounds. I went from a thirty-eight waistline to a thirty-three. I went from wearing an extra-large shirt to a large. I was pescetarian for about three years meaning I did not eat meat, only seafood. I believe that my relationship taught me to stop playing the victim and be the change that I wanted to see. I realized that no one was going to feel bad enough for me to follow my vision for me. No one was going to feel bad enough for me to make me lose weight. I had to take the steps necessary in order to go after my destiny and become a better Emmanuel. I can remember sitting in my room almost every night talking to Angel, having bible studies on Skype and FaceTime, writing down visions and goals, and praying with each other. I felt as if my life had officially started. Do not misunderstand me; I truly enjoyed my childhood. I grew up in a Godly home with loving parents. I grew up with older protective and caring siblings. However, I was not happy with who I was. If I would have listened to people and did not pursue my relationship with Angel, I would still be playing the victim and never moving forward with my life. Always know that God knows what He is doing even in the midst of brokenness, confusion, and persecution.

One of the best decisions I have made thus far is to stay abstinent until marriage. I believe that it is a true blessing to honor God and each other by staying pure until you become one through marriage. Our bodies are the temple of the Holy Spirit. I Corinthians 6:16-20 in the Message Bible says,

> *"There's more to sex than mere skin on skin. Sex is as much spiritual mystery as physical fact. As written in Scripture, "The two become one." Since we want to become spiritually one with the Master, we must not pursue*

the kind of sex that avoids commitment and intimacy, leaving us more lonely than ever—the kind of sex that never "become one." There is a sense in which sexual sins are different from all others. In sexual sin we violate the sacredness of our own bodies, these bodies that were made for God-given and God-modeled love, for "becoming one" with another. Or didn't you realize that your body is a sacred place, the place of the Holy Spirit? Don't you see that you can't live however you please, squandering what God paid such a high price for? The physical part of you is not some piece of property belonging to the spiritual part of you. God owns the whole works. So let people see God in and through your body."

Sex was created as a gift from God to a husband and a wife. Not a boyfriend and a girlfriend. If you are struggling with sexual sin, I encourage you to allow that passage of scripture to soak into your spirit and change the way that you live your life. Do not feel condemned nor guilty because my God is a forgiver. Not only is He a forgiver of our sins, but He is also a forgetter of our sins. Knowing that God is merciful should cause you to sin less, not sin more. Hebrews 10:17 in the Amplified Bible says, *"And their sins and their lawless acts I will remember no more [no longer hold their sins against them]."* – Have confidence in knowing that your body is valuable, you are loved, you are forgiven, you are worthy, and you were created for a purpose.

God did not create you just because He had extra "dust." He created you because He sought a purpose and created you to fulfill it. This is why it is vital to discover your God-given purpose. What is that thing that is burning on the inside of you? What is that thing that you are willing to do every day without being paid for it? – Think of your purpose like a billion-dollar gift that is sitting on a shelf that needs to be revealed and released. There are lives on the line that are waiting for you. We are not waiting on God; God has already done His part. It is time for us to do our part and walk in our purpose daily. Some may ask, "Does this mean I need to quit my job?" – I cannot answer that for you; that is a conversation you have to have with the Holy Spirit. However, I will say that if there is anything getting between you and your purpose, cut it off. It is not God's will for you to live day-by-day as if you do not have a purpose for living.

It is easy for men to get distracted and off course. However, it is vital for us as men to pray and lift each other up. Oftentimes, we are caught up with work, bills, and hardships, but we must push through because there is always someone watching. We have to be the example for the generations to come. Genesis 1:27 in the Amplified Bible says, *"So God created man in His own image, in the image and likeness of God He created him; male and female He created them."* God created us in His own image and likeness. Therefore, our lives should resemble the life of Christ. Our daily goal should be to strive to be more like Christ daily. A man that prays. A man that uses his dominion. A man that knows his power. A man that lifts up not tears down. A man that gives and does not always expect to get. A man that knows his identity in the midst of trouble. A man that stands strong in the Word in the midst of temptation. A man who will lead the generations to come. If you are single, I encourage you to understand who you are as a man of God before you pursue your Queen. If you are dating, searching for your soul mate, I encourage you to stand strong in the midst of your temptations and choose your Queen based off the Word of God, not your feelings. If you are courting, on the journey with the woman who you are going to marry, I encourage you to stay on the right path of purity and abstinence until marriage. If you are married, I encourage you to die to self, daily as you lead your wife and family.

~Dedication~

Otis Gunn, Jr. – Atlanta, GA

Eddie Gunn, Jr. – Atlanta, GA

Malik Adams – Detroit, MI

Elijah Adams – Detroit, MI

Jaden Garwood – Detroit, MI

Killian Gunn – Knoxville, TN

Kelton Gunn – Knoxville, TN

Wilbert Wheeler, Jr. – Knoxville, TN

Jeremy Smith – Spanish Fort, AL

Fred Moore – Clinton Township, MI

Biography of Apostle Dr. Stanley Williams

Apostle Dr. Stanley Williams was born and raised in Blytheville, Arkansas where as a young boy he heard the call of God upon his life. In 1986, Dr. Williams met and married his lovely wife Dr. Bethtina Williams, in Lubbock, Texas. They have been blessed with three sons, Stanley II, Jonathan, and Joshua.

Dr. Williams is a retired veteran of the United States Air Force after twenty-two years of meritorious service. He has been honored to live and travel throughout the world proclaiming the Gospel of the Kingdom to men and women from a diversity of ethnic and socioeconomic backgrounds. He is known and received as a father in the faith to many spiritual sons and daughters throughout the United States of America and across the world.

Dr. Williams has a powerful anointing upon his life to preach, teach and expound upon the Word of God in a uniquely profound yet applicable way, which gives the hearer a rich deposit of revelation and understanding. His teaching has brought significant change and deliverance to many lives, both nationally and internationally. Dr. Williams has been a mentor to pastors and church leaders throughout the United States and abroad for over 30 years. He is widely recognized for having a strong apostolic and prophetic calling that has provided counsel and direction to the lives of many in the ministry, government, and public sectors.

He received his Associate's degree in Business Administration from Mississippi County Community College, a Bachelor's degree in Business Administration from Wayland Baptist University, a Master's degree in Biblical studies, a Doctorate in Ministry, and PhD in Philosophy from FI Christian University.

Dr. Stanley Williams is also a prolific author of several books, including four commentaries. Among his writings are, "But Where Shall Wisdom Be Found," "Upon Approach," "Keys That Govern Success in Life," "A Commentary on the Book of Romans," "Commentary on the Book of Daniel," "Commentary of Hebrews," and "Commentary on the Book of Nehemiah."

God has blessed Apostle Stanley Williams to found Lighthouse of Faith Community Church, Inc., with his wife Dr. Bethtina Williams, which has been a well-diversified ministry that has been far reaching in scope and vision. Since the days of humble beginnings, the ministry at LFCC greatly expanded and ministered to the needs of the communities on a local, national and international scale. The ministry extends its hands through anointed life changing sermons, powerful Praise and Worship, Bible Studies, Children's and Youth Ministries, Men and Women's Fellowships, Singles Ministry, Senior Citizen's Ministry, S.W.A.T. (Soul Winning Action Team), Prison Ministry, Audio Visual Ministries, and Television/Radio Ministries. In the Leadership Training Institute, men and women and women have been mentored, trained and equipped to activate their divine calling to teach, preach and minister the Word of God under the anointing of the Holy Spirit. Over the years, it has resulted in the salvation of thousands of souls in the prisons, local communities and the world.

Today, Apostle Dr. Stanley Williams lives in Atlanta, GA where he has founded and planted another work of ministry at Empowering People International Church, Inc. Apostle Williams is committed to reach, disciple, and equip generations of high impact, low maintenance Christians for the kingdom of God.

Personal Profile

Favorite Scripture

Psalms 8:3-9 *When I consider thy heavens, the work of thy fingers, the moon and the stars, which thou hast ordained; What is man, that thou art mindful of him? and the son of man, that thou visitest him? For thou hast made him a little lower than the angels, and hast crowned him with glory and honour. Thou madest him to have dominion over the works of thy hands; thou hast put all things under his feet: All sheep and oxen, yea, and the beasts of the field; The fowl of the air, and the fish of the sea, and whatsoever passeth through the paths of the seas. O LORD our Lord, how excellent is thy name in all the earth!*

Favorite Quote:

"If your actions inspire others to dream more, learn more, do more and become more, you are a leader." ~ John Quincy Adams

Values

I believe that the Word of God is the highest standard that exists in time or eternity. I am fully convinced if an individual follows God's principles they will ultimately achieve their highest destiny. No book has affected so many people and changed so many lives as the Bible. I cherish it, do all I can to obey it, and live as though it is my necessary food. The ills of the world are many, but God has made sure that we have everything that pertains unto life and godliness. He gave us the information it is up to us to utilize it. The word "value" when defined is: "Core *values* are the fundamental beliefs of a person or organization. These guiding principles dictate behavior and can help people understand the difference between right and wrong." The Word of God is a lamp; it lights the way and establish the destination. What more can a man or woman ask from God? This book represents my value system.

Marketable Skill

I am a licensed Insurance Broker specializing in the areas of Life, Health, Annuities, Long and short term products, Medicare as well as Property and Causality Insurance. I am also an author, public speaker and financial advisor.

Contact Information

Email: wgodly@yahoo.com

Business Email: stanwilliamsinsurance@gmail.com

Phone: 850-585-8646

MANHOOD MAXIMIZED

Apostle Dr. Stanley Williams

<u>Vertical Relationship</u>

The primary responsibility of every man is to develop a relationship with God; all other relationships hinge on and find success because of this one relationship. In the book of Ecclesiastes, Solomon articulated this point so clearly. Ecclesiastes 12:13 (KJV) *"Let us hear the conclusion of the whole matter: Fear God and keep his commandments: for this is the whole duty of man."*

In this passage, Solomon cuts through all the fat. He states it is the entire duty of man to fear God and obey Him. There is no higher call than obedience to God; all other relationships are secondary. This idea is also clearly depicted in New Testament Scripture, where Jesus made it clear, that relationship with Him was the primary relationship. Matthew 10:35-38 (KJV), *"I came to turn sons against their fathers, daughters against their mothers, and daughters-in-law against their mothers-in-law. Your worst enemies will be in your own family. If you love your father or mother or even your sons and daughters more than me, you are not fit to be my disciples. And unless you are willing to take up your cross and come with me, you are not fit to be my disciples."*

This same strand of revelation is also displayed through God's relationship with Abraham. In Genesis 22:2, God told Abraham to get Isaac, go to a mountain I will show you and sacrifice him to me. God did not really want Isaac what He wanted to know is if Abraham would obey Him. It is my contention that God wants to bring His *"now I know to every man."* In Genesis 22:12, God told Abraham not to harm the lad, now I know that you fear me.

Genesis 22:2 (Contemporary English Version) ... *"The LORD said, Go get Isaac, your only son, the one you dearly love! Take him to the land of Moriah, and I will show you a mountain where you must sacrifice him to me on the fires of an altar."*

Genesis 22:12 (KJV) ... *"And he said, Lay not thine hand upon the lad, neither do thou anything unto him: for now I know that thou fearest God, seeing thou hast not withheld thy son, thine only son from me."*

The vertical relationship is the most important of all relationships; it is what God wants. If men give God what He wants, He will make sure men have what they need. Matthew 12:30 ... *"And thou shalt love the Lord thy God with all thy heart, and with all thy soul, and with all thy mind, and with all thy strength: this is the first commandment."*

Horizontal Relationships

When we deal with God, we are looking up. But when we are dealing with humans, we are looking across. This is not just a random statement because God has placed Himself in the middle of all our horizontal relationships. If you are a believer, you must realize that It impossible to have a proper relationship with God without effectively managing human relationships. Here is what the Bible says about this issue in 1 John 4:20 *(KJV)*, *"If a man say, I love God, and hateth his brother, he is a liar: for he that loveth not his brother whom he hath seen, how can he love God whom he hath not seen?"*

This leads us back to God, because without a proper relationship with Him, every other relationship is built on preference. Relationship with God affects how a man conducts himself with his wife, with his kids, with his neighbor, and even with his extended family. Every relationship on earth (horizontal) is affected by the vertical relationship with God. Repeatedly, Scripture outlines the need for believers to walk in love. This is something that men must grasp because men represent the foundation of society. The man was created first; therefore, he was and is the primary individual that God is looking to for leadership. I am not saying that women cannot lead; that would be a lie. What I am saying is that the man has a specific role both in the family and in society.

When a man loves God, he learns to think generationally. He does not think self-centered, but rather looks at and is concerned with what his presence means to his family and their future. God is a generational thinker; He always concerned with the seed. Malachi 2:15 (KJV) … *"And did not he make one? Yet had he the residue of the spirit. And wherefore one? That he might seek a godly seed. Therefore take heed to your spirit, and let none deal treacherously against the wife of his youth.*"

God is interested in the next generation. While it is true God loved Abraham, He was interested in Isaac. In like fashion, God loved Isaac, but He was interested in Jacob. God is interested in our sons and daughters; therefore, the man should be there. Men by virtue of the order of their creation carry authority. It is for this reason God did not say that Eve was primarily responsible, but sought Adam saying where are you in Genesis 3:9. Genesis 3:17 shows Adam abandoning his authority. What a shame! *"And unto Adam he said, Because thou hast hearkened unto the voice of thy wife, and hast eaten of the tree, of which I commanded thee, saying, Thou shalt not eat of it: cursed is the ground for thy sake; in sorrow shalt thou eat of it all the days of thy life;"* We will always be left wandering what would have happened if Adam had walked in authority. This is a call for men to take their rightful place of authority; not to use their strength as a bludgeon but to be guides, supporters and teachers.

Am I my Brother's Keeper?

Who is my neighbor? How do my actions affect not only him\her, but also God? This is a potent question and hits the heart of manhood. Society has made men cold. We are troubled by the concept of love because we think it makes us look weak. It has not sufficiently dawn on us that Jesus was a man's man who always walked in love. The strength of Jesus was that He possessed control over His power. There were times when He would be completely silent and then there were those times when He would be very assertive. Jesus understood the when, why and how principle. He was humble, yet strong; powerful yet submissive to God's will. He knew the boundaries and His walk always pleased God.

Men must master the concept of love thy neighbor, because the closest neighbor that any man has is always his spouse. When this neighbor is mistreated, God is offended. He deals with this type of irresponsibility by withholding answers to prayer. 1 Peter 3:7 (KJV) is proof of this: *"Likewise, ye husbands, dwell with them according to knowledge, giving honour unto the wife, as unto the weaker vessel, and as being heirs together of the grace of life; that your prayers be not hindered."*

(Good News Bible) … *"In the same way you husbands must live with your wives with the proper understanding that they are more delicate than you. Treat them with respect, because they also will receive, together with you, God's gift of life. Do this so that nothing will interfere with your prayers".*

The passage listed above clearly talks about damaging the vertical relationship, even though the infraction may not be directly against God Himself. He has so intertwined Himself in human affairs, that a man cannot mistreat another human without angering the God that created him/her. This knowledge is important to men because we need God. Therefore, we must have the relevant information required to protect the most valuable relationship we have.

In Luke 10:29, a teacher of the Law attempted to trick Jesus. He used all the proper language; he was polished and articulate. His problem, however, was not that he did know Scriptures, but that the Author of the Scriptures did not know him. The religious leader asked Jesus what is it I have to do to receive eternal life. Jesus gave answers the man already knew but added His on twist to His response. He asked the religious leader to tell Him what the Scriptures said about the matter, and finished His inquiry with how do you read it? This was a brilliant choice of words, which left the religious leader stumped. The man knew Jesus had just out maneuvered him, but to justify himself said, "Who is my neighbor?" *Luke 10:29 ... "But he, willing to justify himself, said unto Jesus, And who is my neighbor?"* I submit to all men that your neighbor is your wife, brother, friend, son, daughter, fellow believer and whoever else God has created. God is in the people business; therefore, the way you treat people is the way you are treating God. Do not lose God by misunderstanding the horizontal.

The Gathering of Eagles

It has been my observation over my 35 plus years of pastoring and traveling the world that women are going to go to church. The problem with this scenario is that Satan knows the foundation is absent. As men, we can no longer use the excuse that the church is filled with weak men and women. It is high time that we wake up from slumbering. If this is your excuse, then come and show men how to be strong. Live your life among eagles and you will soar like eagles soar.

The Bible says that we should not forsake the assembly. One thing about Satan, he has his scheme down pat. He realizes that lone sheep are very vulnerable; therefore, he loves Christian men who stop coming to church. Whatever your excuse is cut it out; stop being foolish! There is strength in the assembly. *Hebrews 10:25 (KJV) ... "Not forsaking the assembling of ourselves together, as the manner of some is; but exhorting one another: and so much the more, as ye see the day approaching."*

Men, Christian men are forsaking the assembly; this is unacceptable for both God and us. Paul is speaking out in Hebrews 10:25 because this was happening during his time. The man of God stood up to address it before it could become a major problem. We need to get a grip. The church is important to God; it should be just as important to us. It is in the atmosphere of the church that we learn to eat strong meat. It is in the church that we are grounded. It is in the atmosphere of the church that we become sons of God. In the church, we can be held accountable and grow because of it.

I took some time to really look at how Paul mentored Timothy and it left me with the impression that every man needs another man. I am not discussing homosexuality; I am discussing accountability. You can't get this sitting at home in front of the television; you need the assembly. Paul engaged Timothy; he was personal with him. He discussed his strengths, his weaknesses and his potential. Paul gave Timothy direction, something men of this generation sorely need.

There has never been an age where deception has been so high; information moves at the speed of light. The Prince of the power of the air is having a field day because this is his arena. He works through thought and with the free flow of information. The Scriptures make it clear; in the last days, if possible, even the very elect might be deceived. If men ever needed the atmosphere of the anointing, it is now. Matthew 24:24, *"For there shall arise false Christs, and false prophets, and shall shew great signs and wonders; insomuch that, if it were possible, they shall deceive the very elect."*

Satan works in high places; the highest place on your body is your head. The head is the captain and it is in the head, that the soul is housed. Satan knows this and builds his kingdom in high places; he establishes strongholds or houses of thought that are reinforced by pride. In order to combat this type of deception, you need to sit under the Word in the atmosphere of the church.

Ephesians 6:11-12 (KJV*) "Put on the whole armor of God, that ye may be able to stand against the wiles of the devil. For we wrestle not against flesh and blood, but against principalities,* *against powers, against the rulers of the darkness of this world, against spiritual wickedness in high places."*

Our combat is not against flesh and blood but against spirits without bodies. Satan uses *"wiles."* This English word is derived from the Greek word, *"Methodia"* from which we derive our English word, "method." A wile is a strategy that Satan employs to take on or take down a specific individual. I am convinced that just as God has a plan for each of our lives, Satan also has a plan. The question then is, whom you will follow, and what strategy will you use not to be deceived by the enemy? *Wiles: "μεθοδεία methodeia meth-od-i'-ah From a compound of G3326 and G3593 [compare "method"]; traveling over, that is, travesty, (trickery): - wile, lie in wait."* (Strong's Exhaustive Concordance)

The Gathering of Eagles represents the mighty men of God warring for our prophetic destinies, warring for our families and believing God for the best possible outcome. We are maximized; we understand rules of engagement and we are not backing down from the enemy. We understand that we are engaging an enemy who has been around much longer than we have, but we have the great equalizer the Holy Spirit.

God is calling all men back into the house. Remember God is only coming back for those who are faithful. Jesus did not disown the church; He called it "my house." David spoke of gathering with the saints on holy day and spoke of how much joy he experienced in the presence of other believers. This is what men need, a new outlook on the assembly.

Psalms 42:4 (KJV) *"When I remember these things, I pour out my soul in me: for I had gone with the multitude, I went with them to the house of God, with the voice of joy and praise, with a multitude that kept holyday."*

Psalms 122:1*) ... "A Song of degrees of David. I was glad when they said unto me, Let us go into the house of the LORD."*

Notice that going to the house of the Lord for David was a joy, being with the assembly was joy. David was glad to go into the house of the Lord. I want to encourage men to love the assembly, to look forward to the Word, to be excited about being mentored. I want to see the Eagles gather, who are strong men who love God. What a blessing!

~Dedication~

Mrs. Ruth Williams (In Memoriam)

Apostle Bethtina Williams

Mr. Oscar Aldridge

Mrs. Ophelia Aldridge (In Memoriam)

Stanley Davis Williams II

Jonathan Daniel Williams

Joshua Isaac Williams

Bishop Kirby Clements (Inspiration)

Every Man Needs...

Calvin Ellison, PhD

1. A personal relationship with his Creator - God.

2. A mentor.

3. A friend.

4. A protégé.

5. A field of responsibility.

6. A library.

7. A support team.

8. A specific, consistent routine.

9. A problem he is determined to solve.

HELP FOR ACCELERATED HEALING
PRP| STEM CELLS

#1 IN HOLISTIC SPORTS MEDICINE

Dr. Elmore Alexander is considered one of the leading authorities in Bio Cellular Therapies... He specializes in Platelet Rich Plasma (PRP), Stem Cells, Exosomes, Acoustic Wave and IV Therapies for Sports Injuries and Anti-Aging Medicine which:

- *Restore Youthful Appearance*

- *Reduce Pain*

- *Repair Muscles & Cartilage*

- *Regenerate Blood Vessels*

- *Improve Nerve Function*

208

RESULTS ARE SO EFFECTIVE THAT SURGERY IS OFTEN AVOIDED.

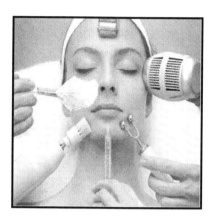

CREDENTIALS

- AFFILIATE PHYSICIAN WITH U.S. OLYMPIC COMMITTEE SPORTS MEDICINE SINCE 1992

- AMERICAN CELLULAR MEDICINE ASSOCIATION

- AMERICAN ACADEMY OF FACIAL AESTHETICS

- AMERICAN MEDICAL ASSOCIATION

CONTACT US: SMARTPLEX ATL
4799 OLDE TOWNE PKWY.

SUITE 201
MARIETTA , GA 30068

678 - 245 – 6777

SMARTPLEXATL . COM

Dr. Elmore Alexander

SmartPlex ATL

Co-Founders: Kenton S. Dazzel & Trista K. Blocker

Business Name: Dazzel Production

Slogan: "Where Your Vision Comes To Life And Dazzles Forever"

Contact Info: 678-505-0370 or 678-469-2871

Website: dazzelproduction.com

Email address: dazzelproduction@yahoo.com

Follow us on Instagram and Facebook @dazzelproduction